"I'm not an alcoholic because..."

Richard L. Reilly, D.O.

LIGUORI
PUBLICATIONS

One Liguori Drive
Liguori, Missouri 63057
(314) 464-2500

Imprimi Potest:
Edmund T. Langton, C.SS.R.
Provincial, St. Louis Province
Redemptorist Fathers

Imprimatur:
+ John N. Wurm, S.T.D., Ph.D.
Vicar General, Archdiocese of St. Louis

ISBN 0-89243-103-2
Library of Congress Catalog Card Number: 78-71358

Cover Design: Linda Harris

DEDICATION

To the
men and women
who allowed me
to use their stories
in this book

TABLE OF CONTENTS

Foreword 7

1. "I'm too young." 11

2. "I can stop anytime I want." 19

3. "I only drink beer." 27

4. "I only drink when I'm depressed." ... 34

5. "I've never had a blackout." 48

6. "I don't drink every day." 56

7. "I only drink when I'm nervous." 72

8. "My drinking just isn't that bad." 81

9. "I'm a woman!" 93

10. "I never miss work." 108

11. "I never really get drunk." 117

12. "An alcoholic is a bum,
    and I'm no bum." 127

13. "I only drink on weekends." 142

14. "I drink because I can't sleep." 150

15. "I just go on a bender now and then." 156

16. "I only drink socially." 166

17. "I always eat when I drink." 178

18. "I'm always able to do my job." 193

19. "I drink only to ease my pain." 205

20. "I don't hide bottles." 214

21. "I drink only to gain self-confidence." . 229

FOREWORD

Will Rogers once said, "I never met a man I didn't like." I suppose I could apply that same statement to alcoholics, but it wouldn't be completely true. I could say without question that I like 99 percent of the alcoholics I've met, particularly if they have some sobriety behind them. When you get right down to it, the major difference between the alcoholic and the remainder of the populace is that the alcoholic is generally a nicer person. Frankly, I've always considered alcoholics as *very* special people.

Some individuals have trouble with this concept of alcoholics being "good people." The major problem revolves around the misconception of just what an alcoholic person is. To many people, "alcoholic" denotes a demented, "skid-row" bum, slumped against a run-down building surrounded by wine bottles, dressed in worn-out, ill-fitting dirty clothes. The alcoholic represents a person observing life through vacant, bloodshot eyes. Anyone who knows anything about alcoholism is very much aware of the fact that this type of alcoholic represents only about three percent of the ten million Americans addicted to the drug.

Most alcoholics are quite normal, overlooking the fact that they have become addicted to a drug. Mothers, fathers, brothers, sisters, aunts and uncles — not your neighbors — but your family; these are the alcoholics. Somewhere along the line, for 101 different reasons, they have crossed the line and have become addicted to the drug alcohol. From that nebulous moment on, they will continue disintegrating until they die as the direct result of ethanol abuse. Only the alcoholic can *fully* appreciate the problems that are created by alcohol abuse. The rest of us are merely spectators in the inevitable tragedy.

Over the past 8 years, I have personally supervised the detoxification and rehabilitation of over 7,000 alcoholics. For the last 5 years, I have devoted 100 percent of my professional life toward that end. My authority rests on that experience.

The stories related in this book are absolutely true. They were told by patients who have come through West Center (Tucson General Hospital's Detoxification and Rehabilitation Center for Alcoholics), or from individuals who are associated with the facility. I've tried to stay away from sensational material. Frankly, I endeavored to use the more "normal" type of stories, because I'm hoping that people with the problem might see themselves and therefore be motivated to seek help. Besides, real-life stories are often better than fabricated ones. Let me assure you that none of the stories used are embellished.

These stories have an obvious purpose. They are meant to demonstrate the typical rationalization with which we must deal on a daily basis. I'm also using the stories as a springboard to educate. Of course, I've changed the names and made a conscious effort to disguise times and places so that individuals could not be recognized.

I've been constantly amazed through the years at the abysmal ignorance of this monumental problem. Alcoholism ranks behind cardiovascular disease and cancer as a major health problem. Eighty thousand Americans die annually as the direct result of alcohol abuse. Industry wastes 25 billion dollars yearly because of ethanol abuse. In spite of all this, the average American has only a kindergarten knowledge of the subject. Another sad fact is that although alcoholism has been declared a disease by the American Medical Association, the American Osteopathic Association, the World Health Organization, and others for almost 20 years, physicians are often less knowledgeable than their patients. It is truly an enigma.

I've been accused of getting somewhat carried away with the subject of my chosen field, perhaps with some justification. I've seen about 10 percent of those 7,000 patients I've been involved with at West Center die from their alcoholism. Most of them have been good people. If you don't mind, I'll keep getting carried away.

September 1978

Richard L. Reilly, D.O.
West Center
Tucson General Hospital
Detoxification and Rehabilitation Center

1

"I'm too young."

Alcoholism respects no age. Many alcoholics disagree with this concept. They feel it takes 10 to 15 years of hard drinking before one crosses that nebulous line into the morass of alcoholism.

I believe there is such a thing as a primary alcoholic, that's one who drinks pathologically from the first experience. I thought that this was pure fiction until I met my first one. The boy was ten. He had been exposed to alcohol six times, and six times he got rip-roaring drunk. A minor miracle saved him from being killed during his last episode. He tried to manage a bicycle and the trip ended with his being thrown over his handlebars. He made a one-point landing on his head.

Teen-age alcoholics are no myth. I've seen my share of these kids. The old adage of taking 10 to 15 years to cross the line is pure unadulterated nonsense. One girl I remember specifically was 14. I remember her age because she had been arrested *14 times* for alcoholism-related offenses. Six months after treatment, she tried to drink "socially" again.

One week later she was back in our facility after chalking up another "drunk and disorderly" charge. After another trip through our program, she became actively involved in AA and she has made it.

Allow me to narrate a quick story about teen-age alcoholism. The story is not unusual. It is a drama that is enacted daily throughout the United States.

Lynn started to drink as a junior in high school. She was and is a charming, intelligent young lady. She was a good high school student, a pompon girl, and steady-dated two of the most popular boys in her school.

Lynn liked the effect alcohol had on her. She said the world looked different; she became less shy. She often became the life of the party with a couple of drinks. Besides all that, peer pressure demanded drinking alcohol. If you didn't drink, you were simply not one of the gang.

Following her junior year, Lynn took a trip to Europe with her parents. There were drinks with meals and drinks at night. She really got to like the stuff, in any shape or form. When the trip was over, she continued to drink heavily. By the end of the summer, she and a friend were knocking off two or three cases of beer a day. Among other problems, she totaled a car.

Lynn suddenly found herself back in high school and facing an alcoholic nightmare. She began drinking in the morning and at lunch. The old facade was there. She was still a pompon girl. She still attended parties, but she was no longer the belle of the ball. From a good student she became a bad student. Formerly respected by teachers, fellow students, and elected to class boards, she suddenly found herself barely passing. She gained 25 pounds. *Question:* At this point in her life, do you think anyone could convince either her or her family that she was an alcoholic? A high school kid full of vim, vigor, and vitality? No way!

Lynn left a party one night, too drunk to drive her car. As a matter of fact, she was too drunk to see the road. After dropping off one of her best girl friends, she promptly ran over her. Her friend spent the next four months in the hospital on the critical list. That shook Lynn up, but not badly enough to stay away from drinking.

The summer between high school and college was nightmarish. She began stealing to pay for booze. The most important matter in life became the next drink. I'm sure that at this point in her young life, you'd still have a hard time convincing her or anyone who knew her that she was an alcoholic.

College away from home was a real joy — the geographic cure! By the end of the first semester she was drinking up to a half gallon of liquor a day. She experienced blackouts chronically. Up to her neck in trouble, she withdrew from school as gracefully as possible — again 25 pounds heavier, bloated, depressed, and totally convinced she was insane.

When your family has money, what happens? That's right — it is off to the friendly psychiatrist. The diagnosis was exhaustion. *You cannot come from a good family and you cannot be 19 and be an alcoholic!* That is simply unacceptable. As is usually the case, she was in and out of psychiatric wards most of that year. After clearing up her exhaustion she was routinely released, in order to go out to drink again. I've heard that same story a thousand times. Lynn began to age visibly and she began to contemplate suicide.

Lynn finally arrived at our treatment center, and while there fell in love with Alcoholics Anonymous. She stayed sober a year and a half. Her whole life made a 180-degree turn; but after that year and a half, she became a little overconfident and got lazy about AA. She left us for a few days. Three days of drinking and she was a complete basket case. After a week or so, she returned for treatment. Now she's back in AA, she's gorgeous, she has self-confidence, and she is full of hope for the future. Her slip was probably therapeutic. She'll make it, *as long as she remembers that she is an alcoholic and works at her sobriety.*

It is interesting to note the fact that the adult populace in the '60s was in a complete uproar over the topic of drug abuse. Drug abuse in the lower class had always been accepted, but all of a sudden, it hit "middle" and "upper" class Americans, and everyone was upset. Mom and Dad were half in the bag from booze, but if

John or Mary came home high as a kite on drugs, God help them!

In the '70s we see a different picture. Sure, many parents are still half in the bag from booze, but now they are more into the drugs. Thirteen billion doses of barbiturates, amphetamines, and tranquilizers were produced in 1976. Valium had to be reclassified. More adults than kids are using drugs. Often they are into both booze and drugs, a tragic combination. The kids, on the other hand, have gone more and more to alcohol as their drug of choice.

A recent study on the West Coast unearthed some very interesting data. No fly-by-night project, it was a professional job by topflight people. The study involved over 2,500 responses and represented an even socioeconomic split. The responses came from approximately one third blue-collar, one third white-collar, and one third professional families.

Surprisingly enough, kids that were in trouble with booze came from all the groups at about the same rate. I wouldn't have voted that way. Only 25 percent of all the groups favored pot over alcohol. Kids from broken homes were in no more trouble than those of more stable environments. I've always felt that the worse the environment, the worse the drinking. Girls were in just as much trouble with alcohol as the boys. My eyeballs widened over this statistic, because the percentage of

15

females to males in our treatment facility seems to be rising every year.

Now these few statistics are rather interesting, but let's take a look at some really hair-raising information. Through the use of skilled questioning, information could be sifted out as to the seriousness of the problems with alcohol. Factors like suffering blackouts, drinking alone, drinking to avoid life's responsibilities, alcohol-induced depressions, drinking to be comfortable with one's peers — all these could be used to differentiate between so-called social drinking and alcoholism. Problem drinkers and alcoholics (I fail to find a distinction between the two) ran in this order: 6 percent (4th to 6th grades); 17 percent (7th to 8th grades); 29 percent (9th to 10th grades); 40 percent (11th and 12th grades); and 42 percent (college).

Now that last statistic does not mean that 42 percent of our college students are alcoholics. What it does mean is that 42 percent of those who drink are already in trouble with alcohol. Six percent of the group in trouble with booze are in grades 4 through 6. How does this compare with national figures? Well, theoretically, 30 percent of the United States adult (over 21) males who drink are in trouble with booze. Using this as a criterion, it would seem that teen-age drinking is more troublesome and progressive than that of the adult. Of course, this is just one study. It is my prediction that further studies, however, will only substantiate the findings of this West Coast study.

One fact that seems to escape most people is that when alcohol is ingested, it is diluted throughout the body. Men usually have more body mass than women. This means that the alcohol consumed by a 100-pound female will be more concentrated than in a 200-pound male. In my experience, women seem to develop brain damage — so often associated with alcoholism — much faster than men do. Younger people usually weigh less. The average person tends to acquire weight with years. Perhaps the higher concentration of alcohol in younger people accounts for some of the escalation of problem drinking in the younger generation.

To say "I'm not an alcoholic because I'm too young!" is ridiculous. Recent data has put that myth to rest. There are about 500,000 teen-age alcoholics in the United States alone. All one needs to do to become an addict is to have adequate exposure to the drug. Age has little to do with it.

Probably the most disconcerting thing about the age factor is the blatant permissiveness of parents in regard to drinking. A parent who may be three sheets to the wind can hardly play Moses to his children. Perhaps this is the basic problem. Whatever the reason, parents all too often allow their children to be exposed to drinking without the slightest supervision. Prohibition laws did not work in our society. It probably is no solution in the home either. Complete disregard for the potentially disastrous effects of alcohol addiction, however, is another matter. Education begins at home. Children are shaped by their parents. Alcoholics come from all kinds of environments, home situations, and genetic strains.

There are no pat answers or solutions. There is such a thing as prudence, however. I doubt if most heroin addicts who are parents would go out of their way to addict their children to heroin. We should at least make it difficult for kids to destroy themselves with alcohol.

2

"I can stop anytime I want."

Sure you can, Charlie! It's just that you never want to stop, right?

Many alcoholics stop drinking for months at a time. However, when they do drink, they tend to lose control quickly. Oh, they can maintain control for a short time, but because of their addiction, they fail sooner or later. It's just a matter of time before the family has to pick up the pieces again.

Alcoholics play this little game ad nauseam. They will give up booze for a week, for a month, maybe a year. They want to prove to themselves that they are not alcoholics. They just don't understand what alcoholism is! Its basic principle is trouble. Ninety million Americans drink without getting into trouble. They can take it or leave it without difficulty. They rarely get into trouble because of their drinking. Alcoholics have problems in many areas of life (their work life, social life, or home life), and all because of their drinking. But, sadly, often they don't get the picture until it is too late.

Some alcoholics are rather comical about their "I can stop anytime I want." They'll knock off the booze for a month and tell everyone in sight. The one they'll inform right away is the one who has blown the most smoke in that direction — the one who has rocked the boat about the drinking problem. "I've been off beer for four weeks now! — as if they deserved a Medal of Honor. They play this little game for years.

Of course, the obvious answer to "I can stop anytime I want" is: "Why don't you stop for good?" If one walks into a lion's den, one gets the picture in a hurry and removes himself posthaste while escape is possible. One does not stick around to get chewed up, and one does not keep going back to get chewed up more . . . unless, unless, unless . . . one is addicted.

The booze is indeed worse than any lion's den. Every time the drinker walks into the den, he or she gets banged around. Boozers know what is going on. Oh, sure, they'll give you a song and dance about quitting tomorrow or next week, and some more of "Remember last year when I quit for three months!" Practicing alcoholics are always quitting. They've quit a thousand times.

Sometimes it is difficult to keep a straight face when exposed to the phony line of the "I can stop anytime I want." An announcement of that type would break up an average AA meeting. After the laughter died, the members would recall how they too had said they could "stop anytime they wanted" — until they finally admitted that they were powerless over the drug alcohol. Sobriety began at that moment. The long climb uphill started at that moment. Sanity returned at that precise instant.

Here's a little story that demonstrates the "I can stop anytime I want to" line. Gil's not all that unusual either. What does stand out, however, is that through all the years he used this line he also managed to play championship golf.

This story is a little unreal, but then life is unreal . . . sometimes. Gil spent 30 years in the United States Navy. During those 30 years, he also played professional golf and rubbed elbows with most of the golfing greats of those years.

Like most good golfers, Gil got started as a caddie in high school. He was good enough to win his state's Junior Championship before he joined the Navy during World War II. He was wounded in the South Pacific in the submarine service, a branch he never left. He was allowed to operate a service golf course while recuperating from his wounds. His game became so sharp, he talked his superiors into allowing him to represent the Navy in some local tournaments. From then on it was a shotgun marriage of golf, booze, and the U.S. Navy.

Gil won so many titles he can't remember half of them. Most of the trophies were immediately turned into cash for drinks. He won a major national championship in the '50s. He led in the first round of the British Open one year, but was disqualified in a later round.

All this time, Gil was a top gun in the nuclear sub business. He turned down commissions many times because he made more money as an enlisted man. He went to great schools such as M.I.T. and Harvard, and pulled down top grades in nuclear math, nuclear physics, and nuclear fission. He taught some of these courses. After serving admirably in the Korean War, he actually was a crew member of a famous nuclear submarine when it surfaced at true North Pole. As a member of that crew he was presented to President Eisenhower. Admiral Rickover was a passing friend.

Gil can tick off every boozer on the present golf tour and give you household names who were then, and subsequently died, alcoholics. He lived as a con man, by his skill on the course and his wits at the bar.

There were good times and bad times in Gil's life, and the bad times were really bad. He was driving across the Mojave Desert once when he went into classic delirium tremens. He pulled over on the shoulder of the road, locked the doors, and woke up several hours later to find the interior of the car a complete mess. There was vomit and urine everywhere.

He's played with the best, and many more who might have been the best if they hadn't destroyed themselves with booze. One of his friends had all the tools: the swing, the temperament, the knowledge, but, unfortunately, a drinking problem too. It forced him off the tour. The last Gil heard of him, he was in prison. It seems he strangled his wife, a woman he adored, in a drunken rage.

Gil has spent a lifetime of "stopping anytime he wants." Surprisingly, enough, he became involved in AA back in 1951. He was "saved." He lived and breathed AA for a couple of years. He had AA in the head, but never in the gut. It didn't last, of course. Then came the suicide bit. The "in and out" of AA continued. He regained consciousness once in a flophouse in Houston, Texas, with cockroaches crawling all over him. The most recent suicide attempt was with carbon monoxide. After that extremely close call, he decided he would stop drinking. It was time! Six weeks later . . . "Oh, hell, one drink won't hurt!"

Gil entered our treatment center as the "last angry man." He was still angry when he left. He has peripheral neuropathy in his legs. He has a continuous tremor that you can't miss. He's 52, but looks considerably older. He still thinks he's into AA, but I wonder. I'm afraid there is still more head than gut. He's back to church. He's had several months of sobriety by now. He is presently an assistant pro at one of the finest and most famous golf courses in the country. Tell me alcoholics are not special people!

Will Gil stay sober? God only knows. He's a troubled soul. Being a golf pro is hardly an occupation that is conducive to sobriety. If, after some 25 years of playing fast and loose with AA, some of that knowledge finally filters down from the head to the gut, at least he'll have a chance. Most professionals — whether in golf, medicine, law, the ministry, teaching, etc. — have a very fine filter. Professionals picture themselves as a cut above the ordinary. Many of them die of alcoholism thinking just that.

One of the reasons why people hang on to that "I can stop anytime I want" theme is pride. Only good persons are able to admit to themselves and their Maker that a drug has the best of them. The prouder they are, the tougher it is. Some of these proud people just can't get past the term "alcoholic." A good friend told me once that his AA sponsor explained it to him this way some 10 years ago. His sponsor said: "You don't have to be known as an alcoholic if that term is offensive to you. From now on I'll just refer to you as a 'miserable drunk' "! Needless to say, he accepted the term "alcoholic," and he has 10 years of quality sobriety in Alcoholics Anonymous.

To me, one of the greatest stumbling blocks to sobriety is material success, whether real or imagined. Any successful person is a natural for the "stop anytime" line. "I'm a success at something; therefore, I, in no way, can admit defeat at anything." Sobriety cannot be built on that foundation.

Professional men and women and their

spouses are often the greatest offenders in this area. Booze is such an integral part of social life that often it gets to be a way of life in itself. Nothing is complete without a drink. A party is nothing without booze. A social function is incomplete without it; no business deal can be closed without it; lunch without booze is gauche.

Professional people are "somebodies." If there is any question in your mind, just ask and you'll catch the tune quickly. A major obstacle in the alcoholism field is that somehow materially successful people feel that they have a built-in immunity. They can't possibly catch "alcoholism." The horrifying fact is they catch it with the same regularity as the rest of the populace. The only difference is that their money protects them from skid row — at least for a while.

It is my opinion that those in a position of authority or who must give professional advice to others are automatically in trouble when "I can stop anytime I want" becomes their motto. Psychiatrists, psychologists, social workers, clergy, family physicians, and their spouses are in great danger unless they are exceptional people. Unfortunately, most picture themselves as "exceptional" people. Many of them go to the grave, bottle in hand, swearing "they can quit anytime they want." It's too bad. Most of them are first-rate people, or at least they were at one time. If, for instance, they had the insight to see how they look in the eyes of others and if they had the humility to join the masses, they'd have the same fighting chance everyone else has. But most of the time, talking to them is almost useless. Treatment is tough sledding. People with money are difficult people to persuade. It takes a lot of patience. To many of them, humility is just another word in the dictionary, not a virtue to be practiced. Too many die slaves of alcohol — saying to the bitter end that they can quit "anytime they please."

3

"I only drink beer."

Several years ago I attended a drug and alcoholism meeting which attracted prominent men and women from a wide variety of professions affected by the subject. I am dumfounded by the separation of the terms "drugs" and "alcohol," because alcohol, of course, is a drug. The "drug addict" is usually pictured as a sleazy, dirty little rat holed up in a filthy tenement housing project; but the boozer who may happen to be a $100,000 corporation executive is just as much a drug addict. I suppose there is some justification, however, in separating the words because: 1) most people just can't seem to get it through their heads that *alcohol* is the *most abused drug* in society; and 2) the magnitude of the alcohol abuse problem is so great that it probably does deserve to be listed separately.

At any rate, this meeting, to which I referred, lasted several days, and, of course, the indispensable cocktail party had to be staged. Sometimes I think cocktail parties have to be thrown at these meetings in order for the people involved in the treatment of alcoholism to demonstrate the fact that they are not alcoholics. If they don't drink, that means that they are alcoholics — recovering, but alcoholics. If they do drink, well then, they are the guys who wear white hats. They are the good guys. It's a horrid little game people play.

During the course of the cocktail party, I bumped into a man representing the beer industry. He was working very hard demonstrating the fact that he was not one of "those alcoholics," and his face looked it. (There's absolutely nothing like attending a three-day meeting on drug abuse and watching an unscheduled demonstration!) In the course of our conversation, he stated unequivocally that one could not become an alcoholic if one drank only beer. Had I been wearing dentures, they would have landed on the floor. He probably picked up the fact that I disagreed with him by the expression on my face and the fact that my voice became louder than any other in the room.

I informed him that 20 to 25 percent of the men and women who had been treated in my alcoholism facility were 100 percent beer drinkers. He countered with the fact that Dr. What's His Name from Ersatz University said that it does not happen. I promptly told him where Dr. What's His Name must keep his head most of the time. About that time, I backed into a friend who runs a facility such as mine in another part of the country. I asked him what percent of the alcoholics admitted to his facility drank only beer. His answer was between 25 to 30 percent. The beer king's face took on a darker shade of red, but I still wonder how much filtered through his alcoholic fog.

Some people seem to think that since the volume of urine produced by beer approaches the quantity of beer consumed, the beer passes right through and has no effect. Of course, the alcohol is pulled out of the gut and taken to the liver for detoxification. This happens to approximately 90 percent of all alcohol ingested. Since the rate of metabolism of alcohol remains approximately the same, the more beer consumed, the higher the blood alcohol concentration. A 160-pound man can detoxify about two cans of beer in three hours. The blood alcohol keeps climbing with additional beer.

One can of beer equals one ounce of hard liquor, and equals four ounces of wine. One shot over the bar is usually one ounce to one and one-half ounces, depending on how much it is watered down and how accurate a pharmacist the bartender is. The rough rule, however, is that one shot equals one twelve-ounce beer. One six-pack equals at least six shots of hard liquor. Anyone who consumes one and one-half six-packs of beer daily is approaching a pint of booze. It is absolutely amazing how many beer drinkers are totally unaware of this simple concept. A typical beer drinker looks down his nose at a person who is drinking a pint of liquor a day as if the "hard" liquor drinker is a real bona-fide "boozer" and he himself is not. It's a strange world!

As a matter of fact, one of the problems that we must deal with in treatment is the individual who decides that the solution to his drinking problem is the big switch from hard liquor to beer. Some even go from Scotch to vodka, to beer, to cheap wine. Pick your combination. Alcoholics deceive themselves when they think that one type of alcohol is less harmful than another. It is absolutely amazing how dumb people can be in regard to their addiction. A school teacher told me the other day that he went this route. He figured he'd actually solved his drinking problem by going from Scotch to beer. Now he laughs about it. Thank God, he is still around to be able to laugh.

This more permissive attitude about beer drinking has probably propelled it into a more dangerous role than hard liquor in the field of alcoholism. Particularly is this true in the case of the young. Young drivers are often involved in traffic accidents and fatalities. Young people are more likely to be beer drinkers. People on the lower socioeconomic scale are more likely to be beer drinkers. Beer tends to "sneak up" on one because it takes a little longer to be absorbed. It doesn't make it less dangerous. A shot hits quickly; beer takes longer, but may be more deadly in the long run.

There's a large amount of calories in beer. Take a look at the label of your favorite brew. It will range from 120 calories to 240 calories. Let's say for argument's sake that the average is 150 calories. A six-pack of beer every day would provide 900 calories, plus the usual food consumed. If an individual needs 2,500 calories to maintain weight, and eats that amount, 900 calories a day would go into fat. Two "six-packs" equal 1,800 calories. It takes 3,500 calories to put on one pound. That 1,800 extra calories per day represents about one pound every other day. Ever wonder where that "beer belly" comes from? Now you know.

Several years ago, when I was in general practice, a woman patient asked me for some pills to help her lose weight. After a good discussion about weight reduction, I gave her a specific diet of 1,200 calories per day along with the pills. One month later she returned for more of the pills, but she hadn't lost any weight. As a matter of fact, she had gained two pounds. On questioning, she swore by all that is holy that she ate only what was on the diet. On further questioning, she admitted she drank a "few beers a day." On still further questioning, the "few beers a day" turned out to be more like a case a day. She consumed 1,200 calories in food, plus around 3,500 more in beer. At that rate, she would have been about three pounds lighter than an elephant in six months.

A recent statistical analysis of per capita beer consumption in the United States shows that there is a higher incidence of intestinal and rectal cancer where beer consumption is highest. New York and Rhode Island reported rates of 80 quarts per capita. Three other states had 26-quart consumption per capita. Intestinal and rectal cancer were more than three times higher in the East Coast states. Another study in New York demonstrated that 35 percent of the males with rectal cancer and 31 percent of the males with cancer of the large intestine were beer drinkers, compared to only 13 percent in a control group. Again, we are merely playing with statistics, but it is interesting.

Many studies have been made relating cardiac damage to beer drinking. Most of the work was done in Germany, and for a long time it was blamed on "trace" metals in the alcohol. Men and women developed sudden congestive heart failure. With the advent of federal research money, more and more information relative to coronary pathology and alcohol consumption has been discovered. I know of nothing good that alcohol does for the heart. Everything so far has been in the "bad news" department. It seems that it is simply the alcohol per se that does the damage. Whether it is ingested in the form of beer, whiskey, gin, vodka, or wine doesn't seem to make much difference. The major factors are the length of time the subject has been drinking and the quantity consumed. So take heart, beer drinkers — the hard liquor and wine drinkers are just as bad off as you are!

I have seen two cases of cardiomyopathy (cardiac muscle damage from alcohol which leads to heart failure) in the past six months — one man and one woman. Both were well off financially. Both were in their early forties. Both were heavy beer drinkers.

Some people consume huge quantities of beer. I have seen patients who routinely consume two cases of beer a day. They must have the world's finest kidneys! Certainly their kidneys should put in for overtime. I see many women who drink a case a day. Amazing as it may seem, they too are quite smug about the fact that they drink "only beer." They suffer the same physical and mental damage that all alcoholics suffer. The brain damage is the same. The intestinal and heart problems may be more. Liver and pancreatic damage is the same. Neurological defects are about the same.

When all is said and done, booze is booze. Beer drinkers just get fatter.

4

"I only drink when I'm depressed."

There is very little that a drink will not make worse. Alcohol, of course, is a central nervous system *depressant.* In spite of this pharmacological fact, people tell me every day that the reason they drink is because they are depressed. If I'm depressed, I'm certainly going to avoid something to make me more depressed . . . unless I'm an *addict* and I can't help myself. Booze just makes depression worse.

Let's take a look at depression and its relationship to the alcoholic. There are three major types of depression: reactive, psychoneurotic, and endogenous. An alcoholic can lock himself or herself into any one of them.

Reactive depression is the most common type of depression, and it is a fairly normal condition. This depression follows a loss. The greater the loss, the greater the depression. One becomes sad, one tends to brood. Some insomnia and loss of appetite are usually present. The alcoholic often parlays normal reactive depression into an excuse for drinking. Some alcoholics blame their drinking on the fact that it is raining. Tomorrow the excuse will be because it is *not* raining. In reactive depression, the grief lasts a few weeks. Even at its worst, this type of depression can be diverted. People can snap out of it momentarily. They can smile briefly. Alcoholics may use this circumstance to drink again or to continue their drinking.

Psychoneurotic depression presents a different case. Here we see weeping, anger, complaining, self-pity, irritability, *preoccupation with loss,* etc. Grief is *flaunted.* Such people deserve plaques for "Martyrs of the Week." They will spend all day telling you how sad and bad they are, but more often than not, they look great. If you told them that they are the finest examples of depression you've seen in a month of Sundays, they would probably take this as a compliment and they'd light up like Christmas trees. Alcoholics can ride this horse to death.

Alcoholics with psychoneurotic depression can be very painful to others. They jump from psychiatrist to psychiatrist, and from family physician to family physician, always with the same line. "Oh, if I could only find out why I am depressed, then I would no longer have to drink!" The depression is used with consummate skill as an excuse to keep drinking. Without this terrible burden of alcohol and with the help of a few years of honesty in AA, they could work matters out; but letting go . . . now that's a job. That depression is tough to give up. They've been beating everyone to death with it for years. It's a tough weapon to abandon.

Psychoneurotic depression *can* spell trouble. Suicide becomes a distinct possibility here. Those who suffer in this way become so histrionic and dramatic that the picture is often confused. One thing is certain — alcohol does absolutely nothing but muddy the water.

One of the major problems that an alcoholic who holds on to the psychoneurotic-depression syndrome has to face is the antidepressant drugs. Physicians are being constantly bombarded by pharmaceutical salesmen and literature suggesting that they prescribe antidepressant drugs. The alcoholic with this problem is in real trouble. The combination of most of the antidepressants with alcohol can be *lethal.* When alcoholics walk into a physician's office and tell him they're depressed, guess what will happen? Alcoholics wear no signs and they are usually not too verbal about their alcohol problems. On the pill they go. I saw one young man die from booze and antidepressants, and that was not long ago.

One of the myths that hangs on and on is that alcohol is a stimulant. I have found it an almost impossible task to bury this one. A shot glass full of gasoline or a shot glass full of boiling water would provide stimulation too. The fact is that alcohol is such a depressant in itself that it can, and often does, cause death. Everyone knows that stimulants help those who are depressed. But alcohol is not a stimulant. Despite this, the psychoneurotic depressant holds on for dear life to the idea that it is.

What can be done with the alcoholic-psychoneurotic depressant patient? Pills certainly aren't the answer! What can a psychiatrist do for someone who's in a fog half the time? Nothing! It takes a good treatment program to break down the wall. He or she has to be convinced that *alcohol* is the primary problem. With AA and follow-up therapy, there's help and hope. AA insists on total honesty. The depression will lift with that honesty. It is painful, but it can be done.

Those of us who treat alcoholics can see with clarity that the depression worn by the alcoholic is often the *result* of alcohol. When sobriety is maintained for a length of time, the depression disappears. It may take months, but it disappears. Mutual problems are talked out with fellow AA members. Aftercare in treatment centers is a monumental boon to these patients. We witness successes daily — but so often, what a mighty struggle is involved in that final surrender!

Endogenous depression presents a huge problem. The alcoholic with this type of depression is quite a challenge. The symptoms that distinguish this individual are many and are seldom classic. One of the most common complaints of the endogenous patient is *fatigue.* A woman, for example, will be worn out only an hour after she goes to work.

Rest seldom helps much. Muscle problems are common. Headaches, backaches, leg aches plague the victim. Muscle pain does not awaken the patient — but starts shortly thereafter. Her *nerves* are bad. Little things cause irritability. Abdominal symptoms are often experienced. A thousand dollars worth of G.I. studies are absolutely negative. Poor appetite is routine. *Weight loss* is common. *Sleep disturbance* also causes problems. Two thirds of the endogenously depressed patients are early morning insomniacs. Sleeping pills help very little. *Inability to concentrate* becomes a problem. People with endogenous depression think about *suicide.* They appear *sad* most of the time for the most incidental reasons. *Decreased libido* is common. Nothing seems to give pleasure. Guilt feelings are often expressed.

Now compare those symptoms with those we find in the alcoholic.

1. *Fatigue.* Alcoholics are frequently fatigued because they don't sleep well. Alcohol ruins normal sleep. With no rest, there is fatigue. Is the fatigue due to alcohol or depression?

2. *Muscle problems.* Alcohol ingestion may cause direct muscle atrophy. When under the influence, alcoholics often fall down steps, walk out windows or in front of cars, fall off ladders or into machinery, sprain

ankles, backs, etc. Orthopedic wards are full of alcoholics. Is all this from inordinate muscle damage or from depression?

3. *Nerves.* Alcoholics have short fuses. Why shouldn't they? Their nerves have been sedated each day by the booze they drink. When alcohol is metabolized, then there is no sedation and the nervous system comes alive. Alcoholics overreact to even minor altercations. Everything upsets them. Depressed patients, or alcoholics?

4. *Abdominal symptoms.* Alcoholics are often genuinely ill with gut pain. Bleeding from gastric ulcers, small gut damage, esophagitis, liver disease, pancreatitis — these show up in a documented pathology very frequently. Now and then, however, we find no reason for the pain. Is the pain from depression or subclinical gut damage?

5. *Weight loss.* In spite of the caloric content of most alcoholic beverages, many alcoholics suffer from weight loss. They do not eat well. They have damaged intestines so they do not absorb their food well. They do not take vitamins. Many have liver damage. Many have pancreatic damage. (The enzymes necessary to digest food come from the pancreas.) Without these enzymes active in the intestines, the food is not absorbed. Is the weight loss from the

depression or the direct result of physical damage from booze?

6. *Sleep disturbances.* Alcoholics seldom sleep well. Alcohol plays a horrible role in disturbing sleep patterns. It may be one year *after* elimination of ethanol before good sleep returns. This indicates something physical, not mental. Is the symptom depression-related or alcohol-related?

7. *Inability to concentrate.* Did you ever see how attentive alcoholics are when they come off booze? They're hyperkinetic; they can't sit. They're restless, they have tremors, their pulse is fast. Everything is in high gear, including their minds. Do you think they can concentrate? Not on your life! Do they get over it quickly? No, not for weeks, sometimes months. This inability to concentrate — is it caused by depression or alcohol?

8. *Thoughts about suicide.* The suicide rate for alcoholics is 60 times that of the rest of the populace. Sure they despair, and they often do more than think and just talk about suicide. Depression or booze?

9. *Loss of libido.* Alcohol causes physical damage to the nerves that supply the genitals. Eight percent of all male alcoholics become impotent. Fifty percent of those who become impotent suffer a

permanent loss here. Loss of libido —
depression or alcohol?

10. *Sadness.* Ten or fifteen years of leading
    anything but a productive life would make
    anyone sad. Alcoholics rarely have much
    to be joyous about when they are drinking.
    Is the sadness due to booze or depres-
    sion?

Alcohol certainly complicates matters. Take
the characteristics of endogenous depression
and apply them to any alcoholic withdrawing
from ethanol. The term "alcoholic" could
easily read "endogenous depression." On the
other hand, one could look over the shoulder
of the psychiatrist and pen in "alcoholic"
whenever he used "endogenous depression."
The problem is that many of his endogenously
depressed patients have never tasted alcohol,
and many others have had no semblance of a
problem with alcohol during their lifetimes. It
does get very confusing.

The accepted treatment for endogenous
depression is the tricyclic antidepressant
drugs. Theoretically, a clinical trial on these
drugs should differentiate the alcoholic from
the "depressed" patient. But look what
happens. We are told to use a potentially lethal
drug (when combined with alcohol) to differentiate between an endogenously depressed
patient and an alcoholic! You do it. I won't.

The experience I've had with tricyclic
antidepressants in their use on alcoholics

makes me question their value in this area. This would lead me to conclude that alcoholics do not generally suffer from endogenous depression. Their problems are a direct result of booze and not depression.

Is it possible for an alcoholic to suffer from endogenous depression and alcoholism at the same time? Anything is possible. Perhaps, if all the people suffering from "endogenous depression" formed an organization similar to Alcoholics Anonymous, we would have fewer sick people.

The pathetic cry of the depressed patient is, "I can't help myself." That hurts. Nine out of ten times, many things can be done, but it takes guts to do them. It is not easy. Nothing worthwhile seems to be easy. And just as depressed patients should not be allowed to wallow in their depression, neither should alcoholics be allowed to drown in their drink. If they were thrown in a pool and refused to move their hands and legs, they'd go down like stones. The only crime is in *not trying.*

Therapists often give up in complete exasperation over the depressed patient. Alcoholism therapists give up on alcoholics who can't say anything but, "It's no use, I'll never be anything but a drunk!" That's the easy way out. It requires no work. People with that attitude *deserve* to go down. Only the alcoholic who is willing to work at sobriety will make it. Only the depressed patient who is willing to invest work in climbing out of the abyss will make it. A good example of this is a lovely 58-year-old widow named Marie. She was born of well-to-do, upstanding New England parents. Her father was a banker. She remembers her mother as being sensitive and loving, but never quite up to the social demands required by an ambitious financier. The marriage ended in divorce when Marie was nine. Both her mother and father were alcoholics.

Marie had no problem with alcohol as a young person. She began drinking at age 16, but never became a "social" drinker. She married a New England farmer at the age of 20 — a man quite different from her father. He was kind, forceful, and loving. They enjoyed a good life working the land and raising livestock. They had three wonderful children. Despite 20 years of hard but fulfilling work, the farm failed. Marie's husband went to work as a salesman. Life changed. Farming promoted togetherness. A salesman had to be "on the road." There were weeks of loneliness for both partners. Somehow they both drifted into nightly drinking. These were depressing years for them.

With the heavy drinking came friction; between husband and wife, between three teen-agers and their parents. Typically, barbed insults, quarrels, guilt, remorse, bad scenes became routine. Marie's husband developed a coronary — the first of three. That first coronary scared the wits out of them. They both gave up drinking. They even talked about going to AA, but the stigma of the word "alcoholic" in a small New England community kept them both at bay. Together they made it — they had four great years, but then the curtain fell. Marie's husband died. Within the space of one year, her husband, her father, and her stepfather died. Then her youngest child married and moved to a different part of the country. Marie took a look around and found very little to raise her sinking spirits. The years of "golden retirement," all the planning and hope . . . down the tubes.

The third day following her husband's funeral, Marie decided that she'd had enough. She got blind drunk. Her favorite drink became the next one. A friend dropped in unannounced several weeks later, thereby interrupting a serious suicide attempt. It took her two weeks in the hospital to recover. There, she discovered the ultimate cop-out, that wonderful substitute for booze, the TRANQUILIZER! With tranquilizers, there was no need for the sauce. There was no guilt either, because a physician wrote a little prescription for it. All was l-o-v-e-r-l-y!

Marie moved. The "geographic cure" was on — new friends, new sights, no unpleasant memories. She still carried that searing pain in her gut; she couldn't shake that. She carried that awful grief of her husband's death with her; she wore it like a coat. The harder she tried to forget the memories, the clearer they became.

Five years of miserable existence passed. She overate and gained a lot of weight. Good literature gave way to just reading to pass the time. Music made her sad. A melancholy movie brought despair. She spent hours watching TV programs which she formerly thought were a waste of time. She never left the house. She started projects and abandoned them quickly. Her good looks began to fade. Buying clothes became a chore. After eight such years, the slow retreat became a rout. All through this, Marie did not consume one drop of alcohol.

One fine day, Marie had a heart-to-heart talk with herself that went something like this: "Marie, you poor thing, what you need is a drink! A drink will pick you up and make you feel better. You couldn't handle it eight years ago; but that was eight years ago!" So, she had two drinks with a friend — no problem! The next day she bought a bottle. After that it was three drinks a day — no more. She even slept well. Several days later, she found herself bouncing out of bed early so she could be first in line at the liquor store. She was wiped out totally for six weeks. Ever hear that story before?

Marie drank a little more each day. She started earlier and finished later. Instead of improving, of course, she got worse. She retreated more and more into herself. The only trip from her house was for liquor or food. One Sunday morning, she found herself clutching a bottle of sleeping pills in one hand and a bottle of booze in the other. For some unknown reason, AA popped into her mind.

She called AA. That call is the reason she is still alive.

Through AA Marie ended up in our treatment center. The first few weeks she had the following symptoms: fatigue, muscle cramps in both legs and back, irritability, very little appetite, insomnia, poor concentration, crying jags, tremendous guilt feelings, and a continuous feeling of hopelessness. Her treatment consisted of an educational program about the disease of alcoholism, a whole new insight into Alcoholics Anonymous with daily meetings, a complete work-through of the grief process, which allowed her to *finally* bury her husband, a lot of group therapy and competent counseling with large doses of T.L.C. and understanding.

Marie has been out of our facility for several months now. She's on a weight-reduction program, attends AA several times a week, sees a clinical psychologist every few weeks, is absorbed in several different projects, looks like a million dollars and feels like it too. Is she 100 percent cured? No, but give her time. Marie didn't get sick overnight and she won't get 100 percent well overnight. She has a beautiful disposition, and with the help of the Man upstairs she'll be a winner.

Marie takes no pills — with the exception of vitamins and Antabuse. She's on no antidepressant drugs. Hopefully, she never will need them again. She still isn't sleeping well, but with patience she will. She hasn't slept well for over five years, with or without sleeping pills. Exercise will help more than a chemical. It all takes time.

Marie is the type of woman who makes working in the field of alcoholism worthwhile. The last time I saw her, she was formulating plans to go back and pick up another degree at the University. She doesn't have it made, but she has a load of new friends and a thousand good AA supporters to bank on. The future is bright, if not luminous.

The alcoholic with good, solid AA support gets out of bed in the morning and says: "Thank you, God, for yesterday. Thank you for the great sleep I had. Together we'll make it through today. I'm not looking back, I'm looking forward. Thank you for the gift of this day. With your help I'll make it!" Alcoholics have to make *today* the first day in the rest of their lives.

5

"I've never had a blackout."

Not all alcoholics have blackouts. Most do. Blackouts are simply periods of amnesia that result from drinking. They may last from a few minutes to several hours, to several days. I've never seen any statistics relative to what percent of alcoholics suffer blackouts; but from my experience over an eight-year period in a detoxification and rehabilitation facility, I would have to say that the great majority of alcoholics do experience this particular phenomenon.

When the subject of blackouts is brought up at an AA meeting, it sounds like a "Can you top this?" contest. Blackouts are a nightmare for the alcoholic. What is even more frightening is the fact that John Law holds alcoholics responsible for their actions while in a blackout.

Over the past several years, I have been asked to testify in court no less than seven times for alcoholics who have committed crimes in blackouts. In most instances, murder was the charge. One man killed his best friend. Another robbed six stores in about forty-five minutes. In *all* instances, the accused had absolutely no recall. What is the defense? There is none. Imagine your lawyer standing before the jury pleading that you were in a blackout and did not recall the committed crime. Half a dozen witnesses have testified they saw you do it. Your lawyer says that you are not responsible. You cannot be held responsible! Oh no? All precedents state otherwise. The simple truth is that you really *do* have no recall. You *are* being tried for something you really *do not* recall. You are completely innocent. You also *do not* have a prayer.

When I list the symptoms of alcoholism to a group of people, blackouts receive a prominent place. But most budding alcoholics respond with, "Doesn't everyone have blackouts?" Really, most problem drinkers feel that it is totally *acceptable* conduct. Having blackouts is like catching a cold. Everyone has a cold now and then. "Anyone who drinks has blackouts; it's normal!" I'm quite serious, the average alcoholic operates under a huge cloud of ignorance and misconceptions.

There's another group of alcoholics who will look at a list of ten symptoms of alcoholism and work one to death. "Ahah! I've never had blackouts! All alcoholics have blackouts, therefore I am not one of those alcoholics!" But missing one symptom hardly excludes one from the club.

Not too long ago, a man who came through my facility told me this story. I found it rather typical and worth recording. The man's name is Hal. He is 35 years of age, reasonably intelligent, rather handsome, and in his own rough way, very likable.

Hal's first blackout occurred in high school. In his senior year, his father found him in the back seat of his car at 10 a.m., on a Saturday morning, after a night's fun and frivolity with the other young lions. His father wasn't exactly thrilled over it, but he let it slide. Hal found out later that a friend had driven him home. He also found out that he and the friend had a rather lively conversation all the way. This was the first clue that his drinking was different.

Hal spent several years in the Army after high school. He acquired a reputation for being able to hold his liquor. It became quite apparent that he could drink his buddies under the table and still see that they got home. He tended to be a binge-type drinker and reserved the booze primarily for weekends.

After the service came a good job, good money, and the good life. His binges started coming closer together. Hal began to worry a little about the drinking, but not enough to quit. After taking stock of the situation, he came up with the inevitable conclusion that what he really needed was a good woman. Marriage would settle him down and his drinking would no longer be a problem. So he got married. The marriage lasted five years. His binges not only came progressively closer together, but they lasted longer. They sometimes lasted for a week. He lost his job. As a matter of fact, he lost several *good* jobs. His blackouts became more frequent too. His wife finally got fed up. Five years of heartache was enough for her! She took off.

One summer Hal spent several days planning a gorgeous weekend at the beach. Just before he left, he had a few drinks at a local pub. Being the gregarious type, he picked up a local lovely on the spur of the moment and then headed east. He drank all the way. The last thing he remembered was a sign that read: "Welcome to Connecticut!" He went into a blackout.

The girl filled him in on what transpired in the blackout . . . 24 hours later. He had driven all the way to Boston without complication. After registering at the hotel, he left their room to get a bottle. He drove off in his car but returned in a cab. He had the bottle, but now he hadn't the slightest idea what happened to his car. An entire day was missing. Out of the blackout now, he began to look for his car. He found it four blocks away from the hotel, decorated with tickets, compliments of the Boston police. After this episode, he was so concerned that he sought out a psychiatrist. He was admitted to the hospital for two weeks' observation. He was heavily sedated with drugs during that hospitalization. At the end of the two weeks, he was informed that his problem was strictly emotional in nature. Three weeks later, he was drunk again.

Hal began to operate in an alcoholic fog a good part of the time. But this did not stop him from working. In fact he got a promotion! He became a supervisor in an auto plant. Eventually, however, he lost that job too because of his booze problem. Alcoholics are not famous for job stability. In *any* work force, six to eight percent of the employees will be alcoholics.

Hal met a woman who *didn't drink.* Solution number two coming up! It worked for a while too. Marriage was heavenly bliss for several months. Hal didn't touch a drop! But then he started to try to drink socially again. It wasn't very long before the binges resumed. On one memorable occasion, he planned a second trip to the beach. He left on a Friday night, but before embarking, he thought the least he could do was have a few for the road. He woke up Monday morning at the beach, under the Boardwalk at Seaside Heights. He had no shoes, no wallet, no watch, no car. Sand fleas had feasted on his body. During this blackout, he had been thrown out of most of the bars in the area. He had no recollection of the long drive to the beach or anything that happened over the 50 to 60-hour period. Somehow, he got his act back together and reported back to work.

Things were getting bad. His friends at work were getting tired of covering for him. His marriage began to come apart. At no time did anyone — his friends, fellow workers, wife, family, employers — ever mention the word "alcoholic."

Hal started drinking another Friday night and went into a blackout. When he came to, it was Sunday evening. He was standing up in a booth in a well-known bar making a fool of himself. The bar was filled with people, most of whom were laughing and jeering at him. That was painful.

When all else fails, the alcoholic will take the "geographic cure." He picked up and left. Hal and his family headed West, where, of course, everything would be different . . . new job, new friends, but, unfortunately, the same old problem. Only a short time later the same scene was repeated. There was trouble at home, trouble at work, trouble with what social life could be mustered.

Hal told me that he learned more about alcoholism in one day at our treatment center than he knew existed. After three weeks, he knew a lot about himself too. When he left, he had the respect of his family and friends. His eyes were clear and he stood taller. I don't think Hal is going to be a winner though, and I'll tell you why. I wasn't convinced that he was completely sold on AA when he left. Oh, he was attending meetings, but still I wonder how much sifted down from his head to his gut. He was taking Antabuse, but I don't think that is enough. If he took Antabuse and attended AA several times a week for two years or so, then he'd make it. I felt a little uneasy about Hal. He may not have had his last blackout.

Blackouts vary. There are no hard and fast rules. The duration and intensity of the blackout periods tend to fluctuate with the intensity of the drinking. There must be a million stories associated with them. I've heard a thousand tales of people going to airports, having a couple of drinks before taking off, and ending up in Junction City, Nowhere, sleeping it off. More people have lost their sobriety in airports. I guess there's something about all those strangers, off to strange places . . . lots of lovely people. "One drink won't matter!"

I have a good friend who happens to be an actor and an alcoholic. He has had many blackout episodes, but one stands out. During his drinking days, he finished a picture in Santa Fe, New Mexico, and then took off with some of his buddies for Tucumcari, New Mexico. After two days of celebrating, the buddies returned home. My friend was just warming up. The last thing he remembered was crossing into Texas. At that time, he knew exactly how much money was in his possession: $145.69. He woke up in a hotel room that he had never seen before. He was physically ill and shaking violently. He sent down to the lobby for a paper and found out he was in New Orleans. He had lost five days.

The bellboy assured him that his car was in the parking lot. He also brought up the usual fifth to help "settle the nerves." When enough booze was consumed to stop the shakes, he took inventory, because it suddenly hit him that he was probably broke. This was not the first time he had been through this scenario.

The immediate problem was to get out of the hotel.

It took quite a bit of booze to get up the courage to check his assets. To his surprise, he found bills in his wallet, shirt and coat pockets. Everywhere he looked he found money. When he added it up, he had $687.22. To this day, he hasn't the slightest idea where the money came from. It was one of the few blackouts with a happy ending.

I know of one real estate salesman who sold ten houses while in blackouts. He received checks in the mail, and he hadn't the foggiest idea why the money was being paid to him. On checking with his company, he was astounded to learn that he not only sold the houses, but he hadn't made an error!

Probably the worst fear harbored by the alcoholic is that deep dread of checking the fenders one morning and finding blood all over them. Don't think that it doesn't happen! Fifty percent of all auto accident fatalities are alcohol-related.

Yes, most alcoholics have blackouts, but a *few* escape this affliction. It is only one of many symptoms. One symptom doesn't make or break a diagnosis.

6

"I don't drink every day."

I suppose that I've heard the above statement 1,000 times. A 20-year-old male, well educated and reasonably knowledgeable, made that exact statement to me a few days ago. He was perfectly serious! He was in trouble with his drinking, or otherwise he would not have come to see me. As far as he was concerned, however, his drinking was strictly related to circumstances, particularly stress. When such a situation arose, he said he overindulged. He had no trouble at parties, etc., because there was no pressure or stress involved.

He also took pills in the form of Valium and Librium. They were for stress also. He was dealing with his problem by using the Big Three — Alcohol, Librium, and Valium.

Now why do you suppose he came to see me? It's hard to believe it, but he wanted Antabuse. That's right! He didn't want to eliminate *all three*. That would shake his nice little comfortable world! As a matter of fact, when it came down to the wire, he really didn't even want to eliminate alcohol completely.

Indeed, he was quite emphatic about that. He planned to drink selectively. For instance, he wanted to be able to plan for a big party, lay off the Antabuse two weeks previous to the party, tie one on, then go back to Antabuse. He was going to make sure that he didn't drink *every day.* Using his special reasoning, that qualified him as not being an alcoholic.

After I calmed down, I questioned the young man and found out that he really was worried. He was nervous about his family too. He admitted that the male members of his family seemed to be heavy drinkers. Apparently the history was extensive. He was an anxious youth. He had plenty to worry about.

The interesting points in his story are:

1. To him, an alcoholic is one who *drinks every day.*

2. His problem drinking stemmed from "pressure."

3. If he didn't have booze around, he'd use a tranquilizer.

4. He wanted Antabuse so he could drink selectively.

5. He is only 20 years of age.

6. His family history showed positive signs of alcoholism.

Let us take them in order:

1. *An alcoholic is one who drinks every day.*
An addict has to have his drug routinely or he will physically withdraw. When he physically withdraws, is he still an addict? Of course, he is. He's an addict until he's buried. All he needs is his specific drug to set him off.

Alcoholics can stay away from alcohol for weeks, months, or years. When drinking is resumed, trouble starts all over again. It's like a man trying to swim the English Channel while weighted down with lead shoes. Is our friend addicted to alcohol? If not, I'd say he's on his way. Oh, he's not to the point where he has to drink continuously, but he probably will be before long. I know of no alcoholic *starting out* who needs to drink every day. True, most end up that way. The one common denominator in every alcoholic's life is the trouble resulting from the drinking. Trouble comes because of "loss of control."

If drinking leads to trouble in this man's life, the chances are that he is an alcoholic already. Whether he drinks continuously or periodically is immaterial. In my mind, "trouble" is the most critical factor in the diagnosis of alcoholism. Once the fact that his drinking has him against the ropes, the only way out is abstinence, or a premature death. This is something an alcoholic doesn't want to hear. He wants to hear that something, somewhere, will allow him to drink "socially" again.

Hundreds of studies have been made and hundreds more are in the process, substantiating the fact that man can be taught to drink again *with control.* As long as money is available, the studies will continue to be made. Often when one of the study results is published, alcoholics with proven records of sobriety go forth to do battle with the bottle, and all I see are losers. I suppose some win, but I don't know where they are.

One study in California set up a bar in a hospital that caused shocks to those alcoholics who took a drink in a simulated bar. The people who prepared the experiment believe that alcoholism is a learned response to stress. Good luck to them! The great thing about all those magnificent studies is that they always take place in such "everyday" circumstances. What man, for example, would go into a bar and pick up a glass of whiskey that will give him an electric shock strong enough to untie his shoe strings? I'm sure Pavlov's dog would not order another drink after this happened enough times; but adult men and women should be smarter than Pavlov's dog.

I suppose I should be more liberal-minded; but, really, so many of these studies are made in anything but natural circumstances that it is tempting to question the sanity of the people who authorize them. If that sounds unfair to the research crowd, I'd like to have them pick up the pieces of humanity who read about the marvelous results achieved in some of these studies — men and women who promptly sally forth thinking they can drink "socially" again. Headlines scream: "Former alcoholics learn to control their drinking!" "Extra!" "Extra!" — and, of course, it spells disaster, more hurt, more pain.

One of the most recent challenges to the abstinence principle was the Rand Study. The report involved 1,340 former chronic alcoholics treated at some 45 centers throughout the United States. Follow-up reports stated that approximately one third of the subjects remained abstinent, one third were drinking heavily (at least on occasion), and one third were drinking "moderately." They found that the relapse rate among the "moderate" drinkers was no greater than that of the abstainers. They, therefore, concluded that this may be an acceptable goal for some alcoholics.

Parenthetically, the report noted that *those who have repeatedly failed to drink moderately and who have physical complications due to alcohol ingestion should not drink at all.* That last sentence just about negates any value to the study in my mind. Most of the alcoholics I know have spent a good part of their lives trying to drink moderately. They kept failing until they got help or died. I also see few alcoholics who do not have physical complications. So much for the Rand Report. Five people could live a lifetime of luxury on the money spent on that one study.

To my knowledge, almost every conceivable modality has been used to teach alcoholics how to control their drinking or to drink socially. Biofeedback, aversion therapy, avoidance conditioning by itself, avoidance conditioning combined with training in alternative drinking behaviors, stimulus discrimination and self-confrontation, contingency management, chemotherapy, and hypnosis have all been tried. Although the journals are filled with claims of success, my personal experience is that those who try to control their drinking just collect more bruises. The winners achieve 100 percent abstinence, and this, invariably, through Alcoholics Anonymous.

2. *His drinking stemmed from pressure.*

It is difficult to imagine a world without "stress" or "pressure." Every occupation carries stress. There are family stresses, social stresses, business stresses — some worse than others. We learn to live with stress and pressure. It is true that some individuals tolerate very little stress and others seem to thrive on it. The problem with alcohol is that its sedative value is often employed to alleviate pressure or stress. Its users frequently forget it is an *addictive* drug. The habit yields to addiction. The user is over the cliff before he realizes what has happened.

Human nature is such that without stress very little is accomplished. Few runners peak without sharp competition. Educators are having second thoughts about throwing out grading. People are naturally competitive. Competition means stress. Elimination of stress through booze often leaves a human being impotent — in more ways than one.

Is it wrong to take a drink to "unwind"? Of course not. Most people are perfectly capable of using the drug without developing a habit or addiction. Some develop a habit, but it stops there. There is no progression. Nine out of ten drinkers seem to be able to control this practice. However, anyone who consistently uses alcohol to relieve pressure is playing a dangerous game.

Alcoholics who use the "pressure" and "job stress" song-and-dance theme are phony as three-dollar bills. They love alcohol; they use stress simply as an excuse to drink. Getting up in the morning becomes an act of stress. Everything makes them "anxious."

Many other alcoholics merely fall into the habit of using the drug to eliminate the "pressure," and the habit eventually develops into an addiction. I believe a good percentage of alcoholics have gone down this primrose path. Some alcoholics seemingly try to develop the disease of alcoholism. All of us have seen men and women headed toward the cliff. We wave flags, we stand on our heads, we plead, we beg, we cajole — but they never seem to get the message. By the time they do, it is often too late. "Bottle fatigue" has already set in.

Our young friend drinks because of *pressure.* That is the first strike against him. I say it represents a yellow light. I say that it is easy to use this as an excuse to develop a serious problem. His drinking is *unhealthy.*

3. *If he didn't have booze around, he'd use a tranquilizer.*
So, what's the difference? The pills are more respectable. They may cost less, but sometimes that's debatable. One is liquid, one is solid. The result is essentially the same. Most people drink for the effect. That effect may be produced by another type of sedative, usually a tranquilizer. Many a wife will berate her

husband for drinking, while 50 percent of the time her medicine cabinet looks like a well-stocked pharmacy. Parents actually terrorize their children because of marijuana use, while they themselves are routinely taking more dangerous drugs. The fact that they are prescribed by a physician is not the point. Tell almost any physician you are nervous, and you'll get a tranquilizer.

It is a well-documented fact that one out of ten people cannot handle alcohol. Another healthy percent cannot handle any of the other types of sedative medication. Cross-addiction with alcohol is very common. People end up with "altered minds." Anxiety today is probably not any more prevalent than it was 100 years ago. But today we hear about it from all sides. The result is that we are much more aware of anxiety, and, of course, a magic remedy is always available; or at least we are led to believe that it should be. God knows, no one is supposed to suffer any more! Ask any child who watches TV, and he'll tell you there are ten ways to eliminate pain with a different pill. Relief may be found in the medicine cabinet *or* in the liquor cabinet.

Recently I read about a study involving 60 alcoholics, all with symptoms of anxiety. They were being withdrawn from alcohol. Each patient received identical capsules of two different major tranquilizers or placebos (sugar pills) three times a day for four weeks. The chief finding of the study was that there was no real difference in effectiveness between drugs and placebos in treating anxiety and depression. Very interesting!

From all evidence so far, the most prescribed tranquilizers — specifically Librium, Valium, and Serax — seem to share the same mechanism of action as other sedatives, including alcohol. Every now and then, the pharmaceutical companies come out with a new super drug, but after the drums dim, they all turn out to be similar. We thought for a while these "benzodiazepines" had a different chemical basis of action, but as it turns out, they are not that much different. Booze, by the way, is still "king of the hill."

It is interesting to note how many people these days are really into tranquilizers. Alcoholism facilities are called upon more and more to withdraw patients addicted to tranquilizers. The withdrawal is sometimes more difficult because of the psychological addiction and the duration of action of these drugs. Addictive drugs such as Valium, Darvon, Seconal are some of the more popular. AA members are bitterly opposed to the injudicious use of these medications. The opposition springs from the best objective evidence — personal experience. Cross-addiction, particularly in the affluent, is a chronic problem treated in alcoholism facilities. Many alcoholics are erroneously fed pills by unknowing physicians, and nothing but trouble results. Very frequently the prescription is nothing but a feeble effort to please and appease the patient. There's no substitute for time and concern. Certainly a pill is no substitute.

4. *He wanted Antabuse so he could drink selectively.*

Antabuse is a good drug. It was discovered quite by accident back in 1947. Two Danish physicians were working on a chemical for the treatment of worms. One took a substance called disulfiram, and then went to a party where he got deathly sick. The other tried the substance and had a similar experience. Since then billions of doses of disulfiram have been used, and some, like the two Danish physicians, are still challenging it unsuccessfully with alcohol — usually once only, however.

The exact mechanism by which Antabuse acts is not known. We know, of course, that alcohol is picked up by the gut and transported to the liver. The liver breaks down the alcohol to the tune of 90 percent. Alcohol is metabolized to acetaldehyde, then to acetic acid, then carbon dioxide and water. When Antabuse is present in the proper blood level, the reaction is stopped at acetaldehyde. Acetaldehyde accumulation certainly causes some of the more memorable symptoms that result. It has been recently shown that some of the symptoms result from the interference of the function of the involuntary nervous system. This especially applies to norepinephrine, a hormone that keeps the blood pressure up where it belongs, among other things.

Our friend wants to use the Antabuse so he can select special drinking times for himself — which is wrong. Many alcoholics are impulsive drinkers. A year's sobriety can be blown with one loose moment at a party. After an impromptu fight with the wife, a drink can look pretty good. Better yet, pick a fight to set up the excuse — that's always good for a drink! Antabuse eliminates all the Mickey Mouse business. The obsessive drinker is also a good candidate for Antabuse. Obsession or not, the alcoholic has no choice with Antabuse in the system, unless he or she feels in the mood for a fast ambulance ride to the emergency room and is financially able to pay the tariff. How does $100 sound?

I feel that Antabuse should be thought of as insurance. Ordinarily, people would not dream of driving without insurance; they would never think of canceling their life insurance policy or their home insurance policies. Antabuse should be considered as a positive, friendly aid.

Many people tell me that Antabuse is just a crutch. Let me say that when the leg is broken, a crutch is not a bad thing. AA is a marvelous crutch. My alcoholism facility is a substantial crutch. Who needs more than one crutch? Well, alcoholism is a sure, slow death, so grab all the crutches around — Antabuse included.

The one major complaint that I have to deal with in this area is the character who latches onto Antabuse and thinks that's all there is to sobriety. Then Antabuse turns into a *rubber* crutch. People can be sober and *miserable*. In AA one learns to enjoy, love, grow, and be proud of sobriety. Serenity is what is needed; and that is not found in a pill. When Antabuse is used, it should be used as an adjunct to AA. I routinely ask all of my patients to take Antabuse for two years after discharge. Do they absolutely have to take it? No, of course not. It is an individual decision. Many can make it without that help, but some may not. What harm is there in two years of insurance coverage while the tenets of AA are beginning to sink in? It takes years to learn the AA principles. If someone can make it without Antabuse — good — I'm all for it. Frankly, I do not think the reward will be greater for making it with or without Antabuse. The point is that one does make it. When a person learns to swim, it helps to practice for some time to learn the rudiments. I like to see people learn their AA principles, go to a few hundred meetings, gain confidence — and then stop taking Antabuse. Like all people in this field, I want to see everyone make it.

Some people claim that for them Antabuse is a tranquilizer. It is not. Antabuse does cause some drowsiness and lethargy the first week or so in some individuals, but in most there is no reaction. If anything, the tranquilizing action emanates from the confidence that the pill brings when taken once a day. It eliminates the possibility of drinking. Playing bartender, going to parties, business lunches, etc., may result in acute anxiety to an alcoholic with new-found sobriety. Antabuse is quite a comfort.

I marvel at the person who says: "I'll take the Antabuse when I need it!" That's like the person who's drowning in the middle of the lake suddenly deciding that a life preserver is a good idea. Or it's like the man in the middle of an alligator-infested swamp suddenly remembering that he was supposed to drain the swamp. The point is the same.

Now our friend wants to use Antabuse to eliminate drinking *at times.* In no way does he believe he is an alcoholic. And he may not be. To label someone 20 years old as an alcoholic — after one interview — would not be fair. But this young man seems to be going through a lot of agitation for someone who has *no* trouble with alcohol. I haven't had what could be called "raving success" with people who claim they can arbitrarily start and stop their drinking at will. That's what is known as "pinpoint control." Most people who claim that sort of control think "Beethoven's 5th" is a bottle.

5. *He's 20 years old.*

As the sage said, "It's too bad youth has to be wasted on the young." Alcoholics who have been around the block a few times cringe when they see a young person acting out the same scene they went through years before. They want to help so badly, and yet they know at that age so few will listen. It's a helpless feeling. Most of the time, all that can be done is to give advice and hope for the best. It seems that the young have to be knocked down 20 times before they realize they are in a fight. It's very hard to see young people get hurt badly, but it often *has to happen.*

Alcoholics have to be left lying in their own vomit, urine, feces, and blood before they get the message. Unless they are *allowed* to lie there, they will probably *never* make an effort to help themselves. As long as Mommy and Daddy come to the rescue, why get off center stage? Frequently I tell young alcoholics that, in my opinion, they have a bad problem with alcohol, and they may be full-fledged alcoholics already. They smirk back at me. I then tell them to return after they have experienced more pain and sorrow. They are usually back within six months, bruised and battered. *Then* they are ready for help. It is the only way many people learn, young or old.

6. *His family history showed positive signs of alcoholism.*

Genetics and alcoholism have always been subjects of intense interest. The fact that alcoholism (or a predisposition to it) may be inherited has been discussed for many years.

An adoption study reported in Denmark proved fascinating. It involved 55 Danish men separated from their biological parents early in life, where one parent had a hospitalized diagnosis of alcoholism. These children of alcoholics tripled the normal divorce rate. The children of alcoholics also had three times as many drinking problems as a control group.

These *two* factors were the only significant differences found. All right, so it's no absolute proof, but the *probability factor* is high.

Asians can be heavy drinkers, but seldom become alcoholics. Genetic difference may be the reason. I read recently about a group of 48 subjects (24 Europeans, 24 Orientals) who were tested following ingestion of alcohol by exact body weight. The Westerners became relaxed, confident, alert, and euphoric. The Orientals, as a rule, experienced muscle weakness, pounding of the head, dizziness, and anxiety. The Orientals also experienced a sharper drop in blood pressure and heart rate. Acetaldehyde levels were higher. No wonder Asians do not abuse alcohol!

Drinking problems have long been studied in ethnic groups. A quick rundown always seems to end with a long look at alcohol exposure in older civilizations. The Italian is not heavy into alcoholism, but the Northern European is. The effect of alcohol on the American Indian is legendary. Many historians believe that whiskey, not guns and aggressiveness, won the West. Eskimos too have the same problem. Indians and Eskimos *seem* to metabolize alcohol more slowly, but this is disputed by some. It is probably due to genetic differences, which may, in turn, be due to *diet* over hundreds of generations. Alcoholism has become a tremendous health problem among these fine people.

As usual, there seems to be no conclusive evidence of the etiology of alcoholism. There seems adequate evidence to assure that a genetic factor is at work in many cases of alcoholism. There's one area, however, that seems to warrant no argument. Whether alcoholism is inherited or acquired, *it is treatable.*

It is amazing to note how very often the disease of alcoholism runs in families. Ask the next alcoholic you meet. From a practical point of view, every time I interview alcoholics I question them about parents, brothers, sisters, uncles, aunts. Their answers make most of us believers in the genetic principle.

Our 20-year-old friend is worried because he comes from a family of alcoholics. That's a real worry. When one reads the literature, it is enough to produce legitimate fright. This man's father and two uncles are practicing alcoholics. He wouldn't admit it, naturally, but he sees himself in that same role. Sure it is frightening. When he gets it all together, he'll be back. He'll probably be battered, but the next time I see him, he'll have his eyes open. There are many like that young man. I just hope that the injuries won't destroy him before he returns. I've seen many die, much younger than he. They died from the battle wounds of their alcoholism.

7
"I only drink when I'm nervous."

The big problem with this group is that they're always nervous. Everyone gets nervous. If we don't get nervous, we're zombies. But one of the ills of society is that we are led to believe that we are not supposed to get nervous. Anxiety is not acceptable. If we become anxious, then we must pop a pill or drink some booze to put the anxiety to rest. If the cavemen had assumed that attitude, we'd still be living in caves.

But life is hardly tranquil. *No one* has it made. Management thinks the worker has it made. He puts in eight hours and goes home. The worker looks at the executive at ease in his chair and thinks the executive has it made. The wife holds down a job outside and runs the house too. She looks at her husband and thinks he has it made. The husband looks at his wife and says to himself: "I'm the breadwinner." "I'm the anchor." "If my health goes, the family goes," etc. No one has it made. "Not having it made" creates anxiety in a million ways, and anxiety makes us nervous.

A major problem lies in the fact that so many people seem to think that *they* are indeed the big exception when it comes to being nervous. There's nothing like "their" nervous system. Women are particularly vulnerable. Their mother was nervous, and therefore they must be nervous. They do not have to present the "iron-man" image. They can cry, carry on, "be weak" (many of the things that men are simply *not* supposed to do) — in short, it is more acceptable in our society to be nervous if we're females. Many of us simply refuse to believe that others can possibly be as laden with problems and stress as we are. The other person always is better off.

Turn on the tube. Within 10 minutes you'll hear a commercial to ease your tension and make life comfortable. Pills will do the trick. Booze makes life beautiful. There's something to make you sleep, wake up; there's a car to make life easy, a make-up that would make an orangutan look beautiful, or a cereal that is guaranteed to turn you from a 90-pound weakling into an Olympic weight-lifting champion in one week. It is a world of make-believe.

Life is filled with stress. Without stress we'd probably never amount to much. How would we earn a place upstairs? Human nature is such that without someone with a baseball bat standing behind us, we'd move very little. Yet tranquillity is what is shoved down our throats by the advertising media. No one should have stress or worries, they say.

How does alcohol help the nerves? It doesn't. It tears the nervous system apart. Oh, it sedates for a few hours, but the price paid later isn't worth it. There's a rebound phenomenon that keeps a jangled nervous system more jangled. The eventual result is a nervous system that is left in shreds. Alcohol is metabolized quickly. When the alcohol is gone, the drums start. This is precisely why the alcoholic may be reduced to drinking shaving lotion or hair tonic in the morning. The body is depleted of booze, it craves alcohol; the addictive process has taken over. Several drinks later everything is fine; then the process starts all over.

If I received a dime from all those who told me the reason they drink is because of their nerves, I'd be well on my way to a fortune. When I tell them that they'd have to look around a long time before they could come up with a worse drug than alcohol, they look at me like my ears are pointed.

They are totally unaware of that horrendous price they pay for using booze. All they see is the immediate effect, which, let's face it, may do the trick. The salesman is able to make a better pitch, the housewife relaxes and enjoys the party, the husband unwinds after a tough day — those are the good things. If only everyone could limit himself/herself to a couple of drinks! The price paid by temperate drinkers is probably small and relatively insignificant. The problem, of course, is that people get to love that effect; and as tolerance to alcohol increases, it takes more and more booze to get that effect. The process continues until addiction occurs, and then it's abstinence or death.

The "I drink because of my nerves" gang is quite a large group. They can't help themselves because it isn't their fault that they drink. It's their nervous systems that are at fault. They were born with this defective nervous system, you see, and they are completely helpless. That takes them off the hook and allows them not to do anything about their drinking. How very convenient!

Members of the "I drink because of my nerves" group are also great pill takers. Their physicians have no idea how much they drink. Few are warned of the danger of combining both. Some find out too late. Their already deranged nervous systems deteriorate, then they go to the physician and say: "I need something for my nerves!" And indeed they look like it. They perspire easily, they have trouble sleeping, they have heart palpitations, they run high blood pressures, they run fast heart rates, they have trouble sitting still. They are merely reaping the harvest of all that good stuff they've been drinking. Because of their drinking, they are coming apart. Their nerves are raw because of booze. They would get better relief if they drank some more booze, but then they'd have to face the fact that they are addicted. Instead of facing the addiction problem, they push it aside for a while. No one plays that game for long.

Tranquilizers have practically no place in the treatment of the alcoholic. Yet, some physicians insist on prescribing them for alcoholics. The only real value of tranquilizers is in acute withdrawal from alcohol. They play a part then, but only for a few days. Twenty percent of the patients in our facility receive absolutely nothing by way of tranquilizers on withdrawal from alcohol.

What happens to the "I drink because of my nerves" people when they get away from booze? For one thing, they get some of their sanity back. They don't have to operate like they are in a fog. They start to deal with problems on their own. They get back some self-respect. Do they have a brand-new nervous system? Not on your life. They go through hell. Not only do they have to stay away from booze but they have to avoid any mind-altering drugs. That means all tranquilizers, sleeping pills, marijuana, narcotics, amphetamines must be avoided like the plague. They must be avoided not only for a while but for a *lifetime*. If any of these substances are used in the future, they should be used with tremendous respect and knowledge of their potential danger. That's some job. Only the strong make it.

I've never known anyone to get back into pills and *not* get back into booze. I see patients congratulating themselves on being off the bottle, and they are half out of their gourd on the pills. Women, again, seem to have a tougher time with the pill problem. One addiction is quite enough, thank you.

A patient told me recently that she visited her physician for treatment of an upper respiratory infection. She had been out of our facility six months and had been abstinent from alcohol since then. She mentioned this in the course of the visit, but said nothing about being nervous, upset, etc. The physician prescribed for her "cold," but the patient was aghast to discover at the drugstore that he had also written for tranquilizers.

I had a patient not too long ago who drank alcoholically and also was a heavy marijuana smoker. He said he could give up the alcohol, but he needed marijuana for "his nerves" — meaning, of course, he could "control" the marijuana. I told him what I tell all patients: He must avoid all mind-altering drugs or he wouldn't make it. He made it for about one month by totally abstaining from booze but smoking heavy, heavy marijuana. Predictably, he tried social drinking again. He lasted another week. Among other things he was guilty of beating his wife. The man is a well-educated, intellectual snob, and he will probably die the way he has lived: looking for some magic "cure," but in the meantime staying drunk and doing nothing about his sobriety. He's one of the "I drink because I'm nervous" herd.

Here's an interesting question. Did the nerve problem cause the drinking problem or did the drinking problem cause the nerve problem? Who really cares? Can alcoholism cause nerve damage? I say yes. I see men and women shaking so badly they can't drink a glass of water without spilling it on themselves — and this, several days after their last drink. I see people in sheer panic because they swear up and down that bugs are all over their beds and snakes are crawling out of the walls. Yes, I see nerve damage from alcohol!

But let us look at the other side of the coin. Assume the nerve problem caused the alcoholism. It is certainly possible that alcohol sedates a nervous person. It is also possible that because a person doesn't like being nervous that alcohol has a pleasing effect. It is quite possible that because people enjoy the calming effect of ethanol so much they expose themselves to this drug at every opportunity. Through the years, addiction takes place. I'm saying this is not only possible but probable, in many cases.

The trap many people in the "nervous" group fall into is that they can back up and say: "Aha! Something in my deep dark past makes me nervous!" "My emotional health is what makes me nervous!" Wonderful! They have a marvelous excuse to continue to drink and never get well. Can a psychiatrist or a psychologist help anyone who is drinking? The drinking has to stop first. Psychiatric and psychological help may follow. It is surprising how the monumental problems seem to melt away when the patient becomes immersed in Alcoholics Anonymous. Patients don't get sick overnight and they don't get well overnight. It all takes time.

A large problem looms on the horizon for alcoholics who become addicted because of their "nerves." What do you do with the nervous system without booze or pills? There are many, many modalities that can be used to help. Using one and all of them still leaves a big struggle. Sobriety is never easy, but those in this group seem to have their hands full. They have to want sobriety badly and have to be willing to work at it like there is no tomorrow. Lukewarm souls are dead before they get started.

We've talked about AA. People make it without AA, but not many to my knowledge. When "nervous" post-treatment alcoholics get anxious, what better option can they take than attend an AA meeting? The great majority of people there have been through many of the same experiences. It's comforting to be able to sit down with others and discuss common problems. There may be a better way to work through a state of agitation, but I doubt it. There are few towns and very few cities that do not offer several AA meetings every night. Some meetings are held during the day. Where there's a will, there's a way! It's merely a matter of priorities.

Exercise is a great antidote for nervousness. Nothing is more beneficial for sound sleep than a fatigued body. Whenever I mention the fact that I have never seen "nervous" people who have just run a mile, it always draws a smile. The solution is too simple. Think about it nonetheless. Have you ever seen someone drop down and do 100 push-ups and then complain about being nervous? What did people do 50 years ago? They never heard of tranquilizers, and you can bet all of them were not alcoholics.

Relaxation exercises, transcendental meditation, and biofeedback are excellent alternatives to drugs. Many alcoholics have found any one of them far superior and beneficial to taking drugs and achieving an equanimity they never dreamed existed. Anything but pills!

8

"My drinking just isn't that bad."

More often than not, the individual who makes this statement has about as much insight into his/her problem with alcohol as Adolph Hitler had into his character when he waltzed into Poland and Czechoslovakia. We should be grateful for whatever success we can muster with these superior beings. In their own minds, they rank somewhere between St. Francis of Assisi and St. Thomas Aquinas. They simply cannot fathom how anyone could misinterpret their drinking as a problem. They condescend to cast a disdainful look in the direction of alcoholics. They often perceive them as definite moral degenerates and second-class citizens. Unfortunately, they themselves are often worse than the worst, and frequently they die that way.

Women are no shrinking violets in the "my drinking just isn't that bad" department. They minimize their alcohol consumption to two drinks a day — with meals, or perhaps at a party. Of course, it would take two people to lift the drinks.

A few simple rules should be followed when tackling these paragons of virtue. First, never interview them alone. Involve as many people as possible who can nail their hides to the door. Their wives, mothers, sisters, brothers, employers — these are all good resources. These alcoholics can be stood in the rain, led back into the house, and then will stoutly deny not only the fact it is raining but claim it is a beautiful day with the sun shining gloriously.

The second simple rule is to make sure that these subjects are reasonably sober when confronted. These "I'm not that bad" characters are half in the bag so much that they assume this is the natural state of all people. Remember that it makes about as much sense to reason with someone in this state as it does to reason with someone coming out from under a general anesthetic after an operation. Unfortunately, the only time to catch such a person sober is at six a.m.

"Successful Sam" is a good example of the "I'm not that bad" syndrome. He can sit down and tell you all about his buddies who drink more than he does, theorizing that since he drinks less than they do, he's not an alcoholic. The facts are, usually, that the people he refers to *are* alcoholics. Some are hard drinkers who have not yet crossed the line; but most of them are alcoholics, and since misery loves company, they hang out together. Successful Sam has money. Money separates him from the skid-row bum — one drinks Scotch, gin, or vodka; the other wine. But the total ethanol consumption is the same. Country clubs abound with Successful Sams. When they play golf they drink a few after nine holes, and many more after eighteen. They drink before dinner and after dinner, and use just about any excuse available to really do some serious drinking. Their social lives revolve around booze. Their business lives revolve around booze. They are very often miserable people, with miserable family lives — bad husbands, bad fathers, bad businessmen (but they won't admit it). And they get steadily worse. They are drug addicts.

Health often becomes a problem here. Booze traumatizes the central nervous system severely. They don't sleep well, they become chronically irritable, they develop hypertension; they have bad stomachs, and digestion is a problem; they become impatient, nothing goes right. You sit "Successful Sam" down and you rapidly get the picture that he keeps looking around to see who you have in mind when you talk about alcoholism.

"Successful Sams" have wives. The wives, too, are frequently alcoholics. They travel in the same circles. To become an alcoholic, all one has to do is be exposed to the drug. It is surprising how often we find both partners with booze problems. If both partners are not treated, the success rate is nil. If one partner is involved, the other belongs in Al-Anon. The spouse is often as sick as the alcoholic. Alcoholism is a family disease. Every member of the family needs help. Sick relationships develop. Frequently, the same lack of insight that inhibits "Successful Sam" from getting help is also present in the rest of the immediate family. The alcoholic needs treatment. The alcoholic's family needs treatment.

Al-Anon is a beautiful organization developed for the spouse of the alcoholic. I recently treated a patient whose wife has been in Al-Anon for five years. For five years he resisted treatment. With Al-Anon's help the wife hung in there. She could, and probably should, have abandoned ship many times. Al-Anon helped her keep her sanity. It helped her do the right things, and — just as importantly — not do the wrong things. She finally won. He asked for treatment. With a lot of effort, they'll have a beautiful life together. They'll grow. Two lovelier people never existed. Al-Anon does that frequently for people.

"Successful Sam" represents a lot of men and women. The wife shares in the success of the husband and she assumes the same posture. Mrs. "Successful Sam" is again another skid-row bum, separated from that unfortunate group only by her money. More often than not, she is protected by her family and so-called friends until she dies. She falls down the steps, wraps her car around a tree, develops cirrhosis of the liver, chronic emphysema, malnutrition, becomes senile early, or kills herself. The family stands around the grave wringing their hands saying, "Poor Mom" — and the only help they ever gave "poor Mom" was to suggest now and then that she shouldn't drink so much. That's about as effective as suggesting that a heroin addict shoot less heroin.

Professional men and their wives very frequently fall into the "my drinking isn't that bad" category. Doctors, lawyers, clergy, university people (the list could cover pages) — these people represent the intelligentsia, whether assumed or earned. They may or may not make a lot of money, depending on their profession; but intellectually, they are definitely not of the "common herd." There's nothing they cannot control, including their drinking. Alcoholics Anonymous is a group reserved for those vulgar few who have no control. But these intelligentsia have complete control whenever they choose to exercise it. Unfortunately, they seldom choose to exercise their self-proclaimed masterful control.

More often than not, so-called intellectuals would much rather be thought insane, or at least "emotionally unstable," than be considered alcoholics. They wouldn't be caught dead in an alcoholism facility because that isn't socially acceptable. But they end up there, after years of "occasional" visits to mental institutions. They go in and out of general hospitals like they had stock in them.

If you are a physician, an attorney, a clergyman, etc., how could you become an alcoholic? "Really now," you say, "isn't that disease contacted by *mortal* men and women?'' The intellectual rationalizes everything! "I have no family problems. Those two previous divorces were due to circumstances not even remotely connected with drinking. The kids hate me? Impossible! I lost my job because of drinking? No, it was just time to move on. Besides, those people had it in for me.'' What nonsense!

Show such people the Grand Canyon and they'll deny it exists. Most of them will die with a drink in their hands, denying they ever had a problem. Lacking humility, they find it difficult to admit that they have become powerless over the drug. The drug has them pinned to the wall, screaming for mercy. There begins a battle between pride and "guts." For most, pride wins out. The battle lost, they die drunks. That sounds hard. That sounds harsh. That sounds dramatic. I don't care how it sounds. That's the way it is.

I want to relate a story about a man whose "drinking wasn't that bad." I know the man quite well. His life would make a good novel. He isn't just a good man, he is a great man.

Mac grew up in the rough section of an Eastern city where his major problem was survival. His formal education was minimal. One of his brothers was killed in a gun fight with the police. He operated as a "bootlegger" until the age of 21. These were the glorious years of Prohibition when the government tried to legislate the drinking habits of the people.

When Prohibition ended, he and a buddy opened a tavern. Few people understood the liquor business as well as he did, even at that tender age. The business prospered; he married and had three children. He also developed a booze problem, but "it wasn't that bad." His business began to interfere with his drinking, and this in turn caused the disintegration of his marriage. All this happened before the age of 27.

Mac sold his business for $15,000. Now $15,000 in the late 1930s was a nice piece of change. Within three years, he drank up every dime of it. By the age of 30, he was penniless — reduced to skid-row level. It was 1939. War was looming. Mac joined the Army after being turned down by the Navy and the Marines because he looked like the bum he was.

In the Army, he restricted his drinking to weekends because he didn't have an option. He went through Officers Training School, showing up at the camp three days late because he was so drunk he stayed on the train. Along the line, Mac developed consummate skill as a manipulator and con man — traits quite common in addicts.

His war experiences would fill a book. He rose to the rank of Captain. He killed so many men he couldn't possibly remember them all — several in hand-to-hand combat. He was tough. When he had to function, he functioned well. When he went on leave, he didn't come back; he was hauled back. His nickname in the service was "Captain Corkscrew."

After the War, he deposited $32,000 with his Uncle, and took off for the Caribbean. He was in and out of every other jail down there. He spent a month in one. After nearly two years, he was in a bar on a small island one day, and complained to the bartender about the "damn bells." "Hell, mister," the bartender said, "there hasn't been a bell on this island for almost 100 years!" Mac got a little nervous over that. Still his drinking "wasn't that bad."

Two years later, he decided that he'd had enough of beachcombing, and he started home. He made it to Florida and wandered into Georgia. Instead of making it home, he landed in a large Midwestern city. He missed his mark by a mere 1,500 miles — which wasn't too bad for a practicing alcoholic.

He still had about $5,000 left, but he was drinking around two quarts of whiskey daily. He found himself in a plush hotel. Nothing but the best! When his clothes got dirty, he threw them out and brought new ones. He met a girl one night in a bar and decided to get married. To give you an idea how sharp his thinking was, he traveled to the next state to get married, when he could have been married right there in the same city. He was not exactly operating on all eight cylinders. The night he got married, he was involved in an alcoholic brawl. The marriage lasted three weeks. He can't even recall the girl's name. Still his drinking "wasn't that bad."

Finally, his money ran out. He moved from the best hotel in town to a room just off skid row at $10.00 per week. He switched from Chivas Regal to bourbon, then to wine. Three months later he landed on skid row. Suddenly his drinking *was* "that bad."

Having sold everything he owned, he was reduced to the status of a beggar. He begged for money to buy wine. For a place to sleep, he used to climb into crates in which coffins were shipped. He'd pile papers on top of himself and be all set for the night — just Mac and his bottle of 25-cent wine. He sold his shoes for a bottle of wine once — going barefooted in the snow.

Mac told me once that there was a favorite hangout for railroad people not far from skid row. Alcoholics would congregate there every payday. The building was long and narrow like a bowling alley. A huge bar occupied one wall. On payday, the railroad men would line the drunks up like bowling pins at the one end. They would buy a bottle of wine and fling it down the length of the floor. The object was to knock down as many drunks as possible, then watch them fight over the bottle. The sport of kings, right? Mac participated in the scramble many a time. It was a blood bath.

One morning Mac awakened in a psych ward. He had gone into delirium tremens in a flophouse and was brought into the hospital in a strait jacket. He had tried to get out a second-story window in the flophouse. After a week in the ward, he was back on skid row, bottle in hand. But this time was different. A clerk in the hospital had told Mac about AA — he tossed the bottle aside and walked 40 blocks to his first AA meeting.

The meeting was held in a halfway house run by a physician who was a recovering alcoholic. There, Mac learned that he was indeed "that bad" and had been "that bad" for 20 years. He learned, in fact, that he was an alcoholic. He and that special physician became good friends.

Within three years, Mac had more than his self-respect back. He managed and became part owner of two restaurants and a bar. (It was not so strange that he went into the bar business; that was one business he really knew.) He was very active in AA, attending four to five meetings weekly. His business grossed over $180,000 per year, and his equity in the three businesses was over $80,000. Then, of all things, a flood wiped him out. The Missouri River overflowed and completely demolished the buildings. Insurance against floods in those days was practically nonexistent. Mac had good reason to drink, but he didn't. He stuck with AA.

The next three years, Mac worked as a lay Brother in a monastery located in a Southwestern state. One has to say that for my friend Mac. He did get around. He helped run the monastery which specialized in treating alcoholic clergymen.

Having donated his talent at the monastery, he took a job running a state alcoholism program. After about a year, a local politician came storming into Mac's office, protesting vociferously about the treatment Mac's staff had given one of his friends. When Mac found out the man in question was using his facility for drying out, and not for rehabilitation, he had him thrown out. The politician shook his finger in Mac's face and demanded his job. Mac gave him a shot to the jaw, jumped right over his desk and pursued him down the hall and out to the street. Luckily, he didn't catch him. For unexplained reasons, Mac resigned his position shortly after that incident. The politician became governor of the state and then went on to the United States Senate. Mac still holds him with the same high regard.

Mac migrated farther West. He opened another restaurant and bought land. Four years later, when everything was going great, he tried to drink "socially" again. He became lax in AA, and after 10 years of sobriety, he went back to drinking. The "slip" lasted three years. He drank up $60,000 worth of property in those three years.

One fortunate thing happened during that "slip." He remarried — this time to a lovely woman who was a registered nurse. She saw him through his bad times, and they *were* bad. He was drinking three fifths of liquor a day. At one point during that "slip," he had his wife lock him up in his basement. After a few hours, he squeezed through a small window and headed for the local bar. He walked in at high noon, when traffic was heavy — in nothing but a cowboy hat, his underwear, and cowboy boots. The bartender handed him a fifth and implored him "to get the hell out." Mac couldn't unscrew the cap, so he broke the top off on the curb and then sat down grandly to drink the entire fifth. He then returned to his home, and slipped through the basement window. When his wife returned from her job at the hospital, she was rather surprised to find Mac in such good shape. She heard about the incident much later.

Mac sobered up in a halfway house he had helped start in the better years. He became active again in AA. That was eight years ago. He's back at work and the business is flourishing once again. He gets up every morning and thanks God for yesterday's sobriety, and asks for help to get through today. He has personally helped hundreds and hundreds of men and women attain and keep their sobriety. He's an outstanding man. I'm proud to call him my friend.

The world is full of alcoholics who are dying not by inches but by yards, claiming to the bitter end, "My drinking just isn't that bad!" It has often been said that the last one to get the picture is the alcoholic. I'm afraid some alcoholics simply refuse to even pose for it. The addiction to alcohol is such that nothing is as important as that next drink. Taking a good objective look at one's drinking can be frightening. Many simply do not have the "guts" to do it.

9

"I'm a woman!"

Nancy was the third child of lower middle-class parents. In later life she found out that her parents wanted only two children. Her grandfathers on both sides were ministers. Early life was unstable, to say the least. The three children were "farmed out" most of the time. For example, one day she was taken for an afternoon visit to some relatives; later she discovered that her parents planned to leave her there for several months. She remembers that at the age of five she faked a "stiff leg" for over one year, just to get attention. She felt unwanted, unloved, and got fat as a defense.

When Nancy was 12, her parents got a divorce. The father was awarded the children because the mother was a "bad woman." At the age of 13, she was raped by two boys who left her in an alley after telling her they would kill her if she told anyone. A "nice man" found her in the alley in that condition, took her to a park, and raped her again. She got home at three a.m., battered and bruised, with her clothing in shreds. Her understanding father beat her half to death, screaming that she was "a whore just like her mother." She spent the next few days in bed, such was the pain. She informed on the boys and they both received jail sentences. Such was Nancy's introduction to the "joys" of sex.

Nancy's father remarried and they moved to a small town. In high school she became a cheerleader, had the lead in the school play, and received "nothing but A's and B's" in her class work. She was an extrovert's extrovert and loved every moment of it.

In school, Nancy tried drinking, but never really got into it. She simply didn't like the taste of it, and she frankly admits that drinking made her sick. In her senior year of high school the family moved to a big city. Nancy dated frequently. She was also heavily involved in church activities; she says she "got saved" about three times a week. Her sister had to drop out of high school to have a baby, and Nancy felt shocked and disgraced.

Nancy graduated from high school and took the entrance exam for Nursing School. She was accepted as a nursing student, but her father refused to allow her to go. She worked at odd jobs and concentrated on fighting off the males. She was what one would call a "looker." The early rape scene was seared into her mind, however, and she played the part of the "iron virgin."

She went to work as a secretary and moved in with three other girls who were a few years older. Her family did not fight the move. Hurt because they didn't seem to care, she tied one on that first night away from home. She also had her first blackout. The "liberated" woman of 17 all of a sudden found she not only liked booze, she loved it. She got drunk every night. She also turned into a sexual athlete. The only exercise she got was leaping from bed to bed. One blackout lasted for a total of three days. In the midst of this new life, Nancy had a reunion with her real mother for the first time in five years. When her father learned of it, he refused to see or talk to her for months.

Nancy was having such a good time — all the sex she wanted, independence, new clothes — that she felt life wasn't worth it, and she decided to kill herself. This was at the ripe old age of 18! She wrote the usual letters, swallowed 50 aspirin, washed them down with beer, and said farewell to the world. She spent the next five days in the hospital in a coma. One thing she remembered when the ambulance arrived to cart her off; she screamed: "Please, God, let me live!" She survived.

Nancy met her first husband at a party. She was smashed as usual. They were married five months later and their first child was born seven months after the ceremony. The second child came three years later, and the last child nineteen months after that — all girls. Her drinking decreased somewhat while she watched her husband's drinking go from bad to worse. He beat her periodically, and she readily admits that she used to invite beatings so that she could use the contusions and abrasions to get whatever she wanted from him. She actually controlled the whole scene.

The marriage was five years old when the first split came. She immediately started bed-hopping after the breakup. But after two months of freedom, she found out that she was three months pregnant. The child was obviously her husband's, so they got back together for another eight years. At age 30, she weighed 200 pounds and was hooked on diet pills. She finally shook the pill habit, and lost 100 pounds on her own in one year.

The 13-year marriage ended in divorce. Drinking was a way of life for both of them, and the marriage turned into one continuous battle. Booze was the major factor in the breakup. The end of the union marked the beginning of worse boozing for both.

Nancy began waking up in strange beds, remembering nothing of how or when she arrived — more blackouts. Many a morning she found herself away from home and had to call her children and instruct them to get ready for school. Drinking, lying, and cheating became her way of life.

She worked her way to a top position in a woman's dress shop. She also learned how to steal. As a matter of fact, she became quite accomplished. But money seemed to slip easily through her fingers. As a result, she lost custody of her children.

Nancy married several more men, including an underworld character and another lush. She lost her job after a two-week binge, which ended in the airport terminal of Orlando, Florida. She found herself crying in the middle of a crowd — no money, no car, no baggage, no nothing. Her father wired her bus fare to get home.

She finally landed another job selling cookbooks. After her training period in St. Louis, instead of leaving for her assignment, she went on a drunk and woke up again with no money, no baggage, no nothing. It was beginning to be a habit. Naturally she was fired.

Nancy met another woman in St. Louis, and the two of them took off for New Orleans. Within a week, they were sleeping in her car at night, washing up in gas stations, and panhandling for drinking money. Things got so bad, they began selling their blood for drinking money. After six months of running, she finally came back home.

On moving into a home with a friend, she found a "responsible position" as a barmaid. But this turned out to be a disaster. Every night after work she drank until she was drunk.

Nancy married again; her husband was a naïve 24 and she was a knowledgeable 42. She used him and several other males at the same time. One birthday she received five gifts from five different men, all of whom had no knowledge of any of the others. Her life was one monstrous lie. Her drinking continued. She got a job in a department store and managed to steal about $50 a week for drinking money. After a few months, it became more like $500 a week. She gave away much of the stolen goods to her "friends," because "friends" were getting harder and harder to come by. She'd make dates to see her children, get drunk, and then miss the weekend. Of course, she was fired from this job too.

Somehow Nancy got custody of her children again, and then promptly went on welfare. She spent most of her time drinking and teaching her girls how to shoplift. The oldest daughter was busted and placed in a group home. Welfare "dropped" her. She began to "hustle" for survival. Her drinking got so bad, she started to fall off bar stools. One morning she woke up with another woman; she had no recollection of what had happened. She began to wake up with more and more strangers.

At no time did she think she had a drinking problem. She knew her life was *out of control,* but thought it was just one of those things she couldn't stop. AA was suggested to her, but she thought it must be some kind of joke. Once she quit drinking for three weeks and once for two months, but she always went back. She began keeping a diary. One night she wrote, "I've never been happier and had so much!" The following night she tried to kill herself again.

Nancy moved to another state and secured a job for which she was highly qualified. She was hired as a security officer "to control shoplifters." As insurance for the job, she managed to have an affair with her boss.

One morning on her way to work she heard someone on the radio talking about alcoholism. She was under the impression that alcoholics were people who drank out of brown bags and never wore socks. The information shook her up. She stopped drinking — for a whole two weeks. She went out with a tall, nice-looking, well-educated man, had some drinks, and the next thing she remembered was waking up in bed with a short fat bum. She had no recall of what happened in-between. When she came home, she was a bit disgusted. She called AA and asked for some literature for "a friend who drinks too much." After reading the literature, she stopped drinking and began to take Valium. Naturally, she noticed very little difference between the booze and tranquilizers.

Nancy thought her first AA meeting was a put-up job. A woman told her story, and for some reason or other it sounded just like hers. The thing that impressed her most was the look of peace on the faces of the members. She wanted that. Two days later she gave up the Valium.

Through the AA program, Nancy has learned to live her life one day at a time. She has learned to accept responsibility. She doesn't just have sobriety, she has *quality* sobriety. She still has her problems, but she, like most good AA members, has a glow about her that sets her apart. She's happy, and it shows. She hasn't had a drink in four years. Do you know what Nancy does today? She's what is known as a paraprofessional in the field of alcoholism. She is in the business of helping others find sobriety and health and happiness without alcohol. She's no longer a taker, she's a giver. She is a gifted counselor with a heart of gold.

Statistics have demonstrated that the percentage of women alcoholics has risen steadily over the last few years. There are many reasons. Women's lib is one reason. More women working is another. Also the advertising media has made it almost gauche not to have a drink in hand. Certainly it has done nothing to curtail alcoholism. Beer commercials and hard liquor commercials portray slinking females posturing in opulent surroundings. It certainly makes booze look seductive. A more accurate, but less glamorous, portrait would picture a fat, forty, flatulent female, tottering precariously on a bar stool, cigarette hanging from one side of her mouth, looking as though she'd been in a fight and lost, slurping a beer. I doubt if it would sell, however.

Today, girls vie with boys in their use of the beverage alcohol. We are sort of used to seeing boys get into trouble with alcohol abuse. Unfortunately, it seems acceptable to see Junior crocked in his teens because "boys will be boys." But it's still not too acceptable to see a girl crocked; it is hardly ladylike to fall down the steps, glass in hand. Maybe this will change too. Perhaps one of these days, mother will think it is cute for her daughter to come home drunk as a skunk, just like dad cheers on his little mirror image. Hopefully, we're not quite there just yet.

Much of the female drinking is done on the sly. Daddy marches off to work and Mommy marches off to the liquor cabinet. She needs a "nip" to get the old motor running. No one is around to tally her drinks. It is easy to fall into the trap. TV is absolutely deadly. Some people tell me that it seems as though their right elbow is connected to the "on-off" button on the TV. The television set goes on and the bottle comes out. Little mother, sitting around sweating out the latest afternoon soap opera tragedy, can get to be a problem and a half, particularly when little mother has a habit of drinking two beers per episode.

One of the more frightening evidences of the toxicity of alcohol recently discovered is the fetal alcohol syndrome. Some physicians noted the peculiar birth defects in children delivered by women with a heavy alcohol consumption during pregnancy. A recent study included 41 subjects — 30 new ones and 11 previously reported. All mothers were alcoholics. The infants postnatally exhibited *slow growth in terms of length, weight, and head circumference, as well as retarded developmental progress* with mental deficiency. Low IQ, small hand size, joint problems, and heart abnormalities are part of the syndrome. One physician reported that if a pregnant woman consumed two to four ounces of liquor daily, the chances of her delivering a child with fetal alcohol syndrome would be around 10 percent. If over 10 ounces were consumed daily, the chances would run around 74 percent.

Actually the fetal alcohol syndrome is not exactly new. Studies were reported as far back as 1834, 1900, and 1968. The direct cause is not known. Some feel the damage is done by the direct toxicity of alcohol itself; some opt for acetaldehyde, a breakdown product of alcohol; still others say it is caused by a combination of alcohol or acetaldehyde, plus nutritional deficiency. Women who drink heavily seldom eat properly — there's no dispute going on there.

Another study of 23 alcoholic pregnancies came up with a mortality rate of 17 percent. That means 4 out of the 23 women who drank heavily throughout their pregnancies delivered babies that did not survive. A follow-up study on the children who did survive showed that they were intellectually deficient by age 7, with 44 percent having IQs of 79 or below. Fetal alcohol syndrome was found in 32 percent of the children who survived. Remember the uproar over thalidomide? Recall the furor about measles in early pregnancy? I seriously wonder how many men and women are mentally deficient today because of the alcohol consumed by their mothers during pregnancy.

How many women are poisoning their unborn babies right now by drinking heavily? We know with certainty that alcohol crosses the placental barrier with ease, and the blood alcohol in the fetus very closely approximates that of the mother. Newborn babies actually undergo withdrawal symptoms very much like babies delivered by mothers addicted to narcotics. It's quite amazing to note how meticulous pregnant women can be about vitamins, eating, exercise, etc., and yet totally ignore this fact about alcohol and its effect on unborn babies.

It is estimated that one out of every four alcoholics is a woman. I think the estimate is low. Women's lib, because it plays down the traditional wife-mother role, seems to take the brunt of finger-pointing. The feminist movement urges women to enter the male preserves. Females entering bars unescorted used to be frowned upon — it no longer is. Women say they suffer more isolation and depression, also the feeling of being "trapped by children." Some claim they drink because they've had to suppress their ambitions in favor of their husbands' careers. Others claim that they drink *at* their husbands — who do not spend enough time with them. Women's years between 30 and 50 have been reported as the biggest problem years with alcohol.

A major factor in the development of alcoholism in the female is the omnipresent protection game supported by well-meaning but destructive families and friends. Since drunkenness has long been considered "unladylike," many women drink secretly. Also, more so than men, they drink alone. The first knowledge of Aunt Minnie's booze problem emerges when she enters the hospital for gall bladder surgery and goes into delirium tremens following the operation. This secrecy has long kept women in the background in terms of research.

Women very frequently have to be coaxed out of the closet to accept treatment for alcoholism. Many react like they've been caught stealing. They are filled with guilt. They often deny everything to the bitter end. Answer one argument and they come up with two more. They refuse help until it is often too late. Their most formidable enemy is their ever-loving families who, in their ignorance, make it possible for "Mom" to continue her drinking.

You don't want to confront Mom, you see, because she won't like it. Dad won't confront Mom because she'll make life more miserable for him. Mom is not allowed to accept the consequences of her drinking, and the end result is certain death from alcoholism. Mom falls down the steps, takes an overdose of pills, kills herself and five other people in an auto accident, dies of a stroke or a coronary because of her blood pressure which is out of control, or meets death in some other alcohol-related way. The family commiserates with each other when it is too late, and God help anyone who is honest enough to bring up the fact that Mom died a boozer! It is not good form. The result of all this is that only a fraction of female alcoholics receive adequate treatment.

It is interesting to note that the female alcoholic often begins her drinking later than the male. Statistics are somewhat scattered, but I have found this to be true as a generality. The fact that girls drink as much as boys surprises many authorities, and they often refuse to accept it as fact. Regardless, women often seem to develop this problem later in life and progress more rapidly than men. The denial is more vehement and, of course, in the older woman, concealment is more successful.

A recent study in Sweden, involving 71 alcoholic women, stated that conviction for drunkenness is usually a late symptom among female alcoholics. Alcohol addiction was well under way by the time they were admitted for treatment. This is just one more example of successful concealment. Forty-four out of seventy-one women alcoholics arrested and convicted for drunkenness have been arrested and convicted previously. This is a relatively good indication of alcoholism progression.

The double standard may, in a large way, contribute heavily to late diagnosis and treatment of women alcoholics. Drunkenness is "acceptable" for the male, but "immoral" for a female. Did you know, for instance, that in ancient Rome a woman who drank got the death penalty? Taking spirits was equated with adultery. And today social censure is still very much in evidence. Chivalry is not exactly dead, but it *is* rather ill.

Sixty percent of American women still work at home as housewives. The fringe benefits for women workers, such as insurance, worker's compensation, holiday pay, etc., are not the greatest. Some authorities feel that almost half the alcoholics in the United States are women, yet strangely enough only 14 of the 542 programs of the National Institute on Alcohol and Drug Abuse are for women.

Women will often seek help for their alcoholism or alcohol-related problems from doctors, marriage counselors, and clergymen. Few in these professions know enough about the disease of alcoholism. Physicians sometimes do more harm than good. Their patients are often misdiagnosed as being nervous or depressed. Women are prescribed potentially addictive drugs in the forms of tranquilizers and antidepressants. Two thirds of all mood-altering drugs are prescribed for women. Cross-addiction is much more of a problem among women than among men. Too often, women are sent to psychiatric wards instead of to alcoholism treatment centers. Law enforcement officials often drop charges against a female alcoholic in a "spirit of chivalry."

Treatment programs have two major drawbacks for women alcoholics: (1) lack of child-care facilities for mothers undergoing treatment; and (2) lack of job training for the future.

Women alcoholics have a built-in fear of losing their children. Entering a facility voluntarily is an admission of alcoholism. Bigotry, fostered by ignorance, may set the stage for legal action, which could result in loss of children. Relatives may step in, but it is a very sensitive area.

Nine out of ten husbands leave their alcoholic wives, often within the first year. Once finished treatment, women are ill-prepared to go out and fend for themselves. Job skills are often nonexistent. The alcoholic needs all the support in the world to stay away from the booze. Walking out into a hostile environment to struggle for survival, with the additional burden of child support, hardly makes for a winning combination.

Alcoholism is no respecter of genders. All that is absolutely necessary to become an alcoholic is exposure to alcohol. Women become as rapidly addicted as men, if not more rapidly. The saddest fact of all about the woman alcoholic is how long she is allowed to get away with it before enough pressure is exerted to make her do something about it. To my mind, nine out of ten times the fault lies with the family that surrounds that alcoholic.

10

"I never miss work."

Take any company with a work force of 10,000, and you will find anywhere from 600 to 1,000 alcoholics on the payroll, depending on the male-female ratio. The heavier the male ratio, the higher the percentage of alcoholics. Six to ten percent is the quoted figure. Every alcoholic on the payroll costs the company a good 25 percent in wages: missed days, tardiness, accidents on and off the job, hospitalizations for alcohol-related sickness, management-union squabbles — these all add up to billions of dollars every year. Alcoholism is found on all levels. The bigger the salary, the bigger the financial loss to the company.

It's quite pathetic when one takes a cold look at the whole picture. Consider a hypothetical company of 1,000 employees. Let's say that this company employs more males, so they should have about 80 alcoholics. The average wage for our fictional company is $12,000 annually. Twenty-five percent of the salary paid to the 80 employees is going out the back door from alcohol abuse. That runs about $3,000 an alcoholic. And

$3,000 times 80 employees equals $240,000 a year. Alcoholism costs American industry anywhere from 15 to 25 billion dollars annually. That seems astronomical, but it is probably on the conservative side.

Let's face it, the average alcoholic *does miss work*. He or she is frequently sick. Mondays and Fridays are bad days for the "Irish flu." Alcoholics "bury" their parents, sisters, brothers, uncles, aunts, etc., 20 times during their lifetimes. This is probably the salient symptom of the working alcoholic. An average of 21 days of work per year is missed by practicing alcoholics.

Now let's take a hard look at our good friend, Faithful Fred, the alcoholic who *does not miss work*. Faithful Fred would show up for work (and on time!) if he had to go through a mine field, swim the English Channel, and climb Mount Everest on the way. Fred's major claim to fame in this world is the fact that he is *able* to show up. In his mind, that is *the* factor that distinguishes him from the other drunks working for the company. He may or may not drink on the job. He's probably falling into machinery, involved in numerous disputes, does poor work, or at least does less efficient work than he is capable of, and his buddies take turns covering for him; but give Fred credit, he always shows up. His family life may be in shreds, his social life nonexistent, but Faithful Fred rings that clock right on time.

You'd have a tough time convincing Fred he isn't a topnotch worker. As a matter of fact,

Fred has a tendency to work in spurts. When he is in gear, he works like he is possessed by the devil. The problem with Fred is that the spurts get farther and farther apart, just like his periods of sobriety. The most frequent thing they say about Fred is that "when Fred is not drinking, he's one hell of a worker!" There are plenty of Freds hanging onto the ropes, waiting for the retirement bell. No one wants to blow the whistle on them. They are being falsely protected, "killed with kindness" — misdirected kindness — which leads to their destruction. Misguided employees protect Fred until he is beyond the point of salvage.

It is very interesting to talk to Fred. Anytime you allude to alcoholism, he'll say: "I never miss work!" He'll use it like a weapon. You can make a statement like "Did you know that a leading heart specialist recently defined heavy drinking as five or more drinks a day, and that such drinking can cut seven years off a person's life?" If Fred is within ten yards, he'll say, "I never miss work!"

The saddest fact of all is that everyone loses in industrial alcoholism. Granted, Fred is the biggest loser. Not only will booze eventually cost him his job, it will eventually cost him his life. A job is a big factor in one's life. Steal a man's wife and it is serious; steal a man's house and car, it is serious; threaten a man's job, and you have a real battle on your hands. Yes, booze will cost Fred everything sooner or later. If Fred makes $12,000 annually, the company loses $3,000 annually. To a big company, $3,000 a year is probably a drop in the bucket. However, Fred may be a top salesman. Fred may cost his company $30,000 a year, just because he operates at *50 percent of his efficiency.*

I know of a practicing drunk who operated at 50 percent efficiency for many years. He had a Ph.D. in physics. He forgot more than most of the people he worked with ever knew. He showed up half in the bag for years. He had so much on the ball that it took little or no effort to keep up with his cohorts. He operated at a fraction of his capacity — everywhere but at the bar. After about three years of playing this game he got into the usual trouble, and his company forced him into a treatment center. Back on the job after treatment, this man's real potential came to the surface. His work output doubled. He turned out to be the best man in the organization, hands down. That man will be worth millions to the company and they know it. But without an effective alcoholism policy, he could have been fired and everyone would have lost.

Suppose Fred were the president of his company. One mistake in an alcoholism fog and the company president could easily lose millions of dollars. People at the top can become addicted as quickly as people on the bottom, if not more so. For people in top company positions, it is usually "pressure" that causes them to drink.

That pressure may turn out to be deciding what color socks to put on every morning; but to hear the executive tell it, the pressure is invariably intolerable. The man or woman on the bottom of the pile is never allowed this excuse. The executive carries the world on his shoulders; and, as any sane man knows, the world can get pretty heavy — which, of course, calls for a drink. Society somehow condemns the poor broom-pushing slob who happens to be an alcoholic; but it is quite permissive of the man at the top who happens to be an alcoholic. The man at the bottom is a "drunk"; the other man has a "drinking problem." An AA member explained to me this difference between a "drunk" and an "alcoholic." He says the "drunk" is one of those people who do not have to go to those *damn meetings.*

In all fairness, executives are exposed to a lot of temptations. Cocktail parties, business lunches, socializing for advancement purposes, etc. — booze is an integral part of the scene. Those who happen to like booze have a built-in disadvantage. They all think they can handle the stuff. Many find out too late that they can't. By the time they get the message, it's "bye-bye, Fred or Frieda!"

Many people are completely unaware that a minimum of 600 industrial alcoholism programs exist in large companies throughout the United States. Most of them are paper tigers. The company makes a big production of developing a program; after taking a bow, they shove the policy in the desk and promptly forget everything in it.

There are about 50 good programs in the U.S. Sharp industrial alcoholism counselors run them. Alcoholics are picked up early and treated. Are they forced into treatment? Yes, indeed! If you were under the impression that anyone *forced* into treatment wouldn't make it, join the ranks! So was I. It is a myth. Alcoholics know nothing about their disease. Alcoholics know little about themselves. A good treatment program opens both worlds. Aggressive treatment plus long-term AA involvement equals success. Actually what really counts is *how early* in the disease process the treatment begins. The industrial situation is tailor-made for fingering early alcoholism cases. Pick up an early case of tuberculosis and you can gun it down quickly. Pick up an early case of alcoholism and you can gun it down. The trump card is always the job.

Let us say that Faithful Fred happens to work for an enlightened company with a good industrial alcoholism consultant. Fred is not going to be overjoyed when he is told to report to an expert in this field. The higher up the ladder Fred is, the harder it is for him to comply. Fred has been spotted on the basis of work performance. *Work performance, work performance, work performance* – that has to be the cornerstone of a good program. That has to be the basis for a company program.

Everyone seems to think that an industrial alcoholism program must turn every supervisor in the outfit into an expert on alcoholism. Try barking at the moon! It would be 90 years before attitudes change. The only reasonable approach in a program is simply to base all referrals on work performance — not alcoholism, not suspected drug abuse, not because the supervisor thinks Fred is unbalanced. *Documented work performance* places Fred right over the trap door. People can cover so long. Education is directed to personnel *not* to cover for anyone. Education is directed toward supervisors to judge only on work performance.

If booze is the problem, Fred is offered treatment. He has a choice. "There's the door, or there's help — make your choice, Fred!" Cruel? About as cruel as throwing a life preserver to a drowning man. The policy may even stipulate that Fred be given a second chance at treatment. And this is reasonable. If someone has a flare-up of arthritis or diabetes, a second treatment is given. Ordinarily Fred will have two chances at treatment, and that's it. Usually, he will make it the first time. If the symptoms of the disease are discovered early enough, he may have another 10 to 20 years of good work in him — not just good work, but excellent work. If Fred had been allowed to work as an alcoholic, that $3,000 to $30,000 (whatever) would have gone out the old back door.

What about the unions? The sharp ones are literally knocking themselves out getting industrial alcoholism programs into their contracts. The union is there to protect, to save jobs. With treatment, Fred will save his job. With a good program, he would be forced into treatment. Thus the union would help save his job by cooperating with the program.

Everyone wins. Fred wins, the union wins, the company wins.

Why doesn't every company have an industrial alcoholism program? I would speculate the primary reason is ignorance. Ask most company officials about a program, and the answer most likely received would be that they have no alcoholics working for them. There are several things wrong with that answer: 1) As stated earlier, from six to ten percent of the company's work force is actively into alcoholism; 2) information of that type seldom goes *up* the ladder — *down,* but not up (the old buddy system); 3) the company official might be an alcoholic himself; 4) most company officials relegate the problem to an almost insignificant priority. You can talk until you are positively blue in the face and the first step — convincing them that there is a need — is never taken.

Several years ago I had a personal experience in this area. I talked to a plant manager of a company that had 2,500 employees. He sort of chuckled over my suggestion that his company start an industrial alcoholism program. He said that there were no alcoholics in the company. After I explained to him that we had already treated eighteen of his employees, all I got was a long silence — but no action. That was five years ago. We have treated over a hundred employees from that company since — God only knows how many are on the payroll losing money for that outfit. Multiply every alcoholic by $3,000 and you'll come up with a clue. If ignorance is bliss, plant managers must be happy people.

Many unions have assumed the instigator role in the interest of industrial alcoholism. It's ironic that a company has to be forced into something that will save it money; but frankly the unions are just interested in saving individual employees. And it is often this type of muscle that is needed to make management see the light.

As to Faithful Fred, he would have been given treatment 10 years before it became necessary to toss him out of his company if an industrial alcoholism program were in operation. True, it takes expertise to develop and run such a program, but those capable people do exist. Universities are turning out qualified people. And there are many gifted people in the U.S. who may not have the degrees, but they are quite exceptional in this area.

"I'm not an alcoholic because I never miss work!" What nonsense! It's about the same as saying I do not have heart disease because I do not run a high cholesterol. You don't have to have every symptom to qualify in this exclusive club!

11

"I never really get drunk."

You can develop tolerance to almost any drug, including alcohol. You can develop a tolerance for arsenic — I wouldn't advise trying it, but it is possible. Alcoholics usually work for a long time to develop tolerance. "The one who can drink everyone else under the table and then drive the others home — that's the one who will develop into the alcoholic" is a truism. It is humorous — yet tragic — to note how very proud males are of the quantity of alcohol they are able to consume and still function. They frequently broadcast it. But all they are really doing is advertising the fact that they have a maximum potential of developing the disease of alcoholism. Women seldom do this. They don't want to be known as big drinkers. They tend to keep to themselves the quantity they consume, and to minimize their intake when questioned.

If we could only see ourselves as others see us. I recall talking to a man not too long ago who adamantly denied the fact that he ever really got what most people call "drunk."

Being "drunk" to some people means busting up taverns; to others it means being on "cloud nine." At any rate, this man's wife got sick and tired of her husband's ranting and raving all night after his usual bout with the booze. He always denied saying half the things she had to listen to. Finally, she started to put it all on tape. The next morning she'd tell him what he said the night before. He'd deny it. She'd play the tape. Did it make any difference? All it did was to make him angry. He denies his alcoholism to this day.

It is true that there are some people who are able to drink heavily most of their lives and still be able to function. They may be killing themselves physically, but they do function. In a sense I suppose they never do really become "drunk." They develop tremendous tolerance. Their drinking is not *progressive.* It does not go from bad to worse; it just stays bad. They suffer no physical withdrawals when deprived of their booze. They do not lose control when drinking. They are able to have several drinks and walk away from more.

But these people are as rare as the American eagle. I think most of the people who claim "they never really get drunk" are alcoholics. I think they crossed the line years ago and they are kidding themselves. I don't think they kid the people around them all that much, but I think they play a masterful game of peekaboo with themselves.

Ask one of these con men his definition of being intoxicated. It usually sounds like a description of the third stage of anesthesia. When the blood alcohol exceeds 0.1 mg percent, you're legally drunk. But many of these characters have more than one DWI (driving while intoxicated). "How did you get the DWIs, friend?" "Oh, that was just a case of bad luck." Sure it was! Chances are that those DWIs represent one in about twenty times our friend got home while driving his car by using the Braille system.

Here's a story about a friend of mine who never really got drunk. His name is Harry. Harry is a type you'd like the minute you met him. He's handsome, well educated, very articulate, and interesting.

Harry began drinking heavily at 18. He even had blackouts at that age. He spent the first two years out of high school as a guest of the Navy, and he spent almost every cent of his pay on alcohol. The bureau drawer in his room contained more bottles than clothes. Like most alcoholics, he drank only when he was alone or with someone else. Of course, it never crossed his mind that he had a drinking problem.

Harry also put some time in the Merchant Marines, and then he spent five years in the Army. He went in as a Private and came out a Lieutenant, with a chest full of medals and commendations. His drinking was a way of life by then. He had to face a Board of Inquiry once because of "minor incidents" involving drinking, but a good lawyer got him off. He never considered at any time that he was an alcoholic. He just drank a lot and never really got all that drunk. The "fickle finger of fate" just interfered with his life too much.

After the Army, he got a job with a publishing house. By now he drank continuously. He drank himself to sleep nightly. Needless to say, he didn't exactly set fire to the publishing world. Once his mother mentioned AA: Alcoholics Anonymous. But he thought it was some kind of an automobile agency. He "never really got drunk," you see.

Harry had to go to a hospital to dry out. He couldn't recall what his diagnosis was, but you can bet your bottom peso that it wasn't alcoholism. After all, Harry was working. He was well dressed, well read, and he was well spoken. He couldn't possibly be one of *those* people. He rejected AA. He could accept the fact he had a neurosis, but not such a banal thing as alcoholism. Numerous visits to psychiatrists supported this thinking — therefore, everything was lovely. A year later he was picked up as a public intoxicant and sentenced to 90 days on a state farm. It took 15 years, but he was gradually getting the picture. Even the law recognized the fact that, yes, he *did* get drunk. In jail, he began to write seriously. (Curiously, his thoughts turned to O. Henry who did much of his writing while in jail, but *not* to the fact that many top American writers of this century were alcoholics!) After jail, he finally joined AA.

Harry then had five years of sobriety. Reminiscing, he feels that although he attended AA faithfully, he had it in his head but not in his gut. He was "on" the program, but not "in" it.

Without booze to slow him down, he went back to school and picked up a Bachelor of Science degree (with honors). He then completed two years of graduate school. He was also assistant director of a University Writers' Conference. Among other things, he won a tuition scholarship for one of his manuscripts.

But Harry tried to drink periodically again — "social drinking." He taught in a small college, and then in a high school. He lasted all of about one year. During that high school tenure, he had two experiences with delirium tremens. He listened to music coming from the bedposts, conversed with the birds, and tried to ignore unseen voices gossiping about him. At this juncture in his life, he did what most alcoholics do, he mounted his steed and left for another part of the country. Geographic change! Things will always be better somewhere else.

As usual, things didn't get better; they got worse. He became a steady customer of the police department. He had been drinking now for about five years. He worked at odd jobs, got a few bucks ahead, and then went on another bender. The police would pick him up; and after his release he would start all over again. He was reduced to pandering and drinking the wine of other winos. (He himself had too much pride to beg.) Harry was incarcerated so often the police automatically relegated him to the kitchen of the county jail.

He was seated one sunny afternoon on a park bench when the all-time low hit. His tremors were so bad he couldn't even roll a cigarette. He couldn't focus his eyes. He couldn't walk. His only means of identification was a pink booking slip from the county jail. He found himself screaming, "I've had it. God, I need help!" The police picked him up and took him to our treatment facility.

After leaving the treatment center, he lived for some months in a halfway house. For the first time, he systematically went through the fourth and fifth steps of AA. Six months later, he got a job with a florist. Nine months later, he was back teaching high school.

Harry is a gifted teacher. The students love him because he is honest, knows his subject, and he loves his occupation. If you told one of his students, or any of their parents, that a few years ago he was a skid-row bum, you'd have a big fight on your hands. Harry will continue to share his great gift with young people as long as he stays active in Alcoholics Anonymous. If he becomes lazy in AA, he will lose again. Harry is one drink away from a drunk, and another drink will probably land him on skid row. There may never be a second climb out of that gutter.

I suppose some think that Harry's story is remarkable. Those of us in treatment work see it quite often. But some are not as fortunate as

Harry. About a year ago I tried to talk a man into accepting treatment. After an hour or so, I got him to the point where he would come in after the weekend. It was Saturday morning then, and I had made a special trip in to see him.

His story was similar to Harry's. He was a skid-row bum for several years and pulled himself out of the gutter, with help, of course. Few make it alone. Within seven years, he had amassed a fortune. He ran several businesses with holdings all over the country. The first six years he stayed active in AA. The last year, he decided he didn't need AA any more. When I saw him, he had been married a short time to a beautiful woman about 15 years younger than he, and was, incidentally, up to his eyeballs in financial trouble. One year of drinking and his world collapsed. The reason he could not come in was that he had some loose ends to take care of, so his business pressures could be eased. That night he put a bullet through his head.

Hundreds of men and women have told me that they are not alcoholics "because they never really get drunk." Many will die with a bottle in their hands, thinking to the bitter end that they never ever really get *that* intoxicated. You know why this is so sad? Some of these folks are sincere, splendid people who are too proud to take an honest look at their drinking. They stagger through life denying an obvious problem. It is obvious to everyone but themselves. They destroy themselves, their spouses, the lives of their children, their friends — always denying the problem.

Maybe it is a coincidence, but it seems to me that the "I never really get drunk" characters always seem to have money. Without the money, many would be begging on skid row. Because of their money, they are protected. However, as the money goes, so does their protection. Eventually the progression of the disease of alcoholism will demand payment in full.

You know what is tragic about this situation? The families of the "I never really get drunk" group get sucked into a deadly game that eventually destroys everything and everybody. You know something else? Their families deserve it.

Usually, the "I never really get drunk" alcoholic is inordinately proud. Those who surround him — family, friends, employers, clergy, etc. — let themselves be played like a piano. Instead of allowing the alcoholic to take his lumps and bumps as a consequence of his drinking, they rally round and protect him. This, of course, gives him a golden opportunity to continue drinking. The spouse should be in Al-Anon. The children should be in Alateen. The alcoholic must be allowed to pay his dues, to suffer; otherwise, he has no reason to quit. A line must be drawn and ground must be stood. Anything short of this is a big game, and any alcoholic worth his salt will make the others look like rank amateurs. He chooses the game he wants to play. He holds all the cards. The people who allow the game to go on deserve to lose.

An interesting question arises when the group being mocked by an alcoholic refuses to do anything to change things. (They refuse to go to Al-Anon. They refuse to go to Alateen. They reject advice from experts in the field.) The obvious question is, what are they getting out of it? Some spouses take a financial and moral beating from their alcoholic partners. They enjoy nothing better than to play the bleeding martyr. Many a spouse will divorce an alcoholic, only to turn around and marry another alcoholic. They have to be getting something out of it! It's one thing to get bruises, but another thing to beg for them.

It is a fact that many people who surround the alcoholic love the part they play. If you don't believe me, ask them to initiate a change. They won't budge. Secretly, they love to moan and groan. A woman, for example, will like to be singled out: "Poor Mary, she has 24 children. She is raising them in a mobile home. She takes in washing, and works as a waitress 26 hours a day; all Joe does is drink, and he doesn't even admit he has a problem." Nonsense. Mary loves every minute of it, and wouldn't have it any other way. When they say in Alcoholics Anonymous, "Alcoholism is a family disease," that's exactly what they mean.

How does one distinguish between a "hard drinker" and an "alcoholic"? The ranks of "hard drinkers" are filled with the "I never really get drunk" elite corps. Remember those two characters mentioned earlier — progression and loss of control? The "hard drinker" doesn't get progressively worse; the alcoholic does. The "hard drinker" doesn't lose control; the alcoholic does. How some men and women can be exposed to the drug ethanol for years and years in tremendous doses and never develop addiction is a medical mystery. Believe me, they are about as rare as red-headed Japanese.

12

"An alcoholic is a bum, and I'm no bum."

The first drink Dave had as a kid was at age 16. It was Scotch and he loved it. He out-drank everyone in his peer group. From that first drink he knew he was something special in the drinking department. He could hold his liquor better than any of the others. It was the start of a love affair that lasted a long time.

Dave wasn't exactly born with a "silver spoon" in his mouth. As a kid he sold papers, peanuts, popcorn. He always seemed to have something to sell — he did then, and he does now. He was never turned on to school, but he excelled in other areas of life, such as shoplifting, gang fights, and truancy. His family seemed to be always in debt. One day his Spanish teacher — right in front of the class — informed him that he wasn't really responsible for his actions because of his "upbringing." That sort of ended his high school career. He was 17 then.

He got a job as a short-order cook, which wasn't bad, except he knew nothing whatsoever about cooking. He moved in with his boss, a man whose hobbies were women and wine — not particularly in that order. He was a quick study, both as a cook and as a womanizer. It wasn't long before he had a female "friend" pregnant. He paid $75 for the abortion, and celebrated by downing a quart of red wine and passing out shortly thereafter. For some reason, the girl wanted nothing to do with him after that, and he never could figure out why. At the time, he pictured himself as a cross between Errol Flynn and Clark Gable.

Dave was so distraught and crushed by the outcome of this first tragic romance that it took him almost one week to get over it. He was soon in hot pursuit of another girl he'd met while still in high school. She talked him into going back to finish his schooling. He even got a good job as a clerk in a shoe store. One of the fringe benefits was wholesale shoes and socks. His buddies would come in and point out the shoes and socks they wanted. Dave would buy them wholesale, and then sell them to his friends at a profit. He felt the principle was sound, and he used it most of his life. Unfortunately, his employer did not share his enthusiasm about the fringe benefits and Dave moved on (at the employer's request).

To Dave, drinking was no problem. But his father took a dim view of things when Dave got plastered and wrecked the family auto. Several people in the car were hurt. Shortly thereafter, he was invited to move out of the house, but the drinking was merely coincidental in his mind.

The next few years were fairly well taken up with the active pursuit of flying airplanes, working in a retail store, aggressively utilizing his "equity" principle, chasing women, and staying half in the bag. There was still one girl, but she was reserved for marriage plans. The entire drama almost ended one day when he "buzzed" his true love's home, "hot shot pilot" that he was. He very nearly crashed. Of course, it is a handicap to fly when one is completely out of one's gourd on booze.

The girl's parents were crazy about Dave. When he asked for the girl's hand, her father told him to come back when he had $3,000 in the bank. In 1939 that was a lot of money. Seven months later, Dave showed up with $3,000. He was what one could describe as a "wheeler-dealer."

Marriage, as usual, wasn't all bliss. One daughter resulted from the union. Dave seemed to have a lot of trouble with his "nerves." After drinking half the night, he found himself "nervous" the next morning. He visited his physician, and the physician diagnosed his condition as "nerves." He prescribed something to calm him down. His father-in-law suggested about every five minutes that Dave be placed in a "sanitarium." The relationship between Dave and his in-laws became less than harmonious. As far as Dave was concerned, he never missed work; and after all, if he was an alcoholic, he'd miss work.

"Alcoholics are bums." He was anything but a bum.

When World War II erupted, Dave was ready. The service offered two wonderful solutions: 1) the discipline would solve the drinking (problem?), and 2) it would afford him the opportunity to continue flying. He was wrong on both counts. He flunked the physical for the Air Force and landed in the Navy Medical Corps. The service also allowed him to move up from amateur to professional drinking status. Whiskey was $2.00 a fifth as a corpsman, and he had access to Benzedrine. The combination was a new high he could not resist.

When his Division landed in the South Pacific he prepared himself with 100-proof alcohol and Benzedrine. He says that most of his outfit did the same. Dave was wounded and sent back home after five landings. He arrived in the States drunk as a skunk.

After the war, Dave got into the jewelry business. The pay wasn't all that great, but his "equity" principle took care of the slack. He bought jewelry wholesale and sold it on the side. He learned the business well, but the booze kept him from making much progress. The drinking got so bad his wife finally left him. His boss let him know that he wasn't too crazy about his drinking either, and eventually he lost his job with him.

Dave now found himself on skid row in Detroit. He was destitute, but certainly not a bum. Alcoholics were bums. He was neither.

He had a "drinking problem," but he could take care of that anytime he really wanted to. He was still master of his destiny; he was still in command. By no stretch of the imagination was he an alcoholic, because as every sane man knows: "Alcoholics are bums." He got off skid row by reenlisting in the Army for three years.

Dave was sent to a camp in California, and once more he was placed in the Medical Corps. He was attached to a dispensary and spent most of his time selling Benzedrine and 100-proof alcohol. Being the honest soldier that he wasn't, he felt that his name guaranteed the quality of the merchandise he sold. He therefore felt honor-bound to sample all the merchandise.

Dave's wife finally joined him in California. Their child unfortunately contracted polio. This resulted in a hardship discharge from the Army. So Dave went back to Detroit and the jewelry business. The drinking led to the inevitable problem with women, and his wife left him once again. The situation got so bad, he tried the geographic cure. He caught a bus for the Far West.

Arriving with 17 cents in his pocket, he somehow talked himself into a good job in another jewelry store. Six months later, he had enough money to send for his family. Six years later, he purchased his own jewelry store. A few years after that, he bought still another store. He made loads of money. He also drank a lot. He learned from experience that the "bennies" kept him going during the day and the booze did an admirable job at night. By 1961, he was bankrupt.

Dave went back to work for another jeweler. As usual, he had things going on the side — anything for a fast buck. He found himself dealing with some questionable characters closely allied with the underworld. Things went from bad to worse again, and he decided he had "had it." One night he took 100 Librium tablets along with a fifth of Scotch. He woke up in the Veterans Hospital with a huge headache. They advised him to get out of the business world.

Dave actually tried to go back into the medical field. He spent eight months in a nursing school. He learned quickly that nursing provided few financial rewards. Soon he entered the "loan shark" business. Back to "booze and broads."

Dave could parachute into the Sahara Desert and have a business going in a month. He shifted from "loan shark" to jewelry salesman. His specialty was turquoise, his territory, the whole United States. He bought turquoise from the Indians and sold to Macy's, Gimbles, and many other large department-store chains. No slouch, he always went first class — blond secretary and all. When he came home after one trip, he found himself divorced, with all finances tied up by John Law. "That's simply not fair!" said Dave, so he got even by going on a drinking binge that ended in Portland, Oregon, on skid row again.

He went through the agony of delirium tremens in a flophouse.

On skid row he learned to beg, but he would never admit to being a bum, because bums were alcoholics. He got a job picking cabbage and cucumbers, and saved enough money to buy a suit. After three weeks, he had another job as a jeweler in Portland. In December of 1973, Dave had a coronary. The next month, he was out of the hospital, drinking like there was no tomorrow. Within a few weeks he was back in the hospital. This time he had a massive coronary infarction. He was told to find less stressful work. Never was the alcoholism mentioned. He left for the desert once more.

Dave expected to be welcomed like the prodigal son when he arrived home. Instead he got the treatment he deserved. So, he got even with them all by going on a three-month binge. Sick, sick, sick, he was placed in a state-supported drying-out facility. He was dragged there by his nephew and son-in-law. They had found him dead drunk in a fleabag motel. After a few days, he was transferred to a halfway house.

There, Dave met a young man whom he trusted and liked. The man was a counselor working on a Master's degree in the field of alcoholism. He pointed out to Dave that it was not necessary to live the way he did. He had two choices: He could kill himself with booze, dying with a bottle in his hand, or he could quit the booze. He was an alcoholic but he could make it — all he had to do was try. The only crime was in *not* trying. Dave finally surrendered. He admitted *he was an alcoholic.*

Three months later, Dave found himself not only sober but attending a six-month counseling school in Colorado. The school was set up to develop nonprofessional counselors in the field of alcoholism. Dave loved it. That was three years ago.

What does Dave do today? He works with alcoholics — mostly skid-row men and women. He gives of himself; he gives 110 percent. He's helped hundreds and hundreds of people gain their sobriety and, with it, their self-respect. That's his life's work. He's still a wheeler-dealer, but now he wheels and deals with lives. To him, sobriety is hardly a bed of roses. He doesn't make much money. He still keeps a sideline going — I suppose he can't help himself there — but he keeps his head on straight. With three years of sobriety behind him, he'll make it. He gets his highs from helping others; he used to get his highs from ripping them off. He never realized it, but he spent almost 40 years ripping himself off.

"An alcoholic is a bum." Isn't it interesting how we stereotype people? Estimates vary as to the actual percentage of alcoholics that end up on skid row, but the highest I've ever heard was five percent. In spite of this, many, if not most, people seem to harbor this misconception that an alcoholic has to be a skid-row bum. It is a dangerous concept. Often, in the skid-row bum, we see the "bottom of the ladder" alcoholic; but such a person usually started descending the ladder many, many years before. The tragedy, as always, is that the alcoholic, man or woman, could have been turned around — if only someone or something had intervened. "Of all the sad words of tongue or pen, the saddest are these . . . it might have been."

Let's examine Dave's story and see what we can learn from it. In every life, there is much to be gleaned. Alcoholics are immensely interesting people. They tend to be kind and loving and *giving* . . . particularly if they become good AA members. Dave's story has a wealth of information.

Dave was probably a primary alcoholic. He drank alcoholically right from the beginning at age 16. Looking back, he readily admits that his drinking was different. Booze affected him differently. He could drink his buddies under the table right from the start. He loved alcohol and the effect it had on him; it wasn't a gradual thing, it was instantaneous.

Dave was in trouble with his drinking. Ninety million people are able to imbibe without trouble. Their drinking is comfortable; it does not result in trouble and heartbreak. When I say Dave drank alcoholically, I mean that his drinking got him into trouble. He was in trouble in school, at home, and with society. If you asked him about that right now, he'd have to toss it around in his mind for about two seconds. His drinking spelled trouble from the start and pursued him until he finally surrendered.

Booze costs money. "Booze and broads" cost more money. Dave had to make money at a pretty good clip. He told me once that through the years he probably made close to a million dollars; but, because of alcohol, most of it slipped through his fingers.

It's depressing for any alcoholic to look back too much. "A day at a time." "Thank God for today's sobriety!" That's AA. When you need money, it is easy to develop some shabby methods of getting it. "Gray areas" become attractive. Fringe elements become interesting. Dave got caught up and learned the game well.

He wrecked the family auto — drunk. He was asked to leave his family. His marriage was a failure. He blamed most of it on his "nerves." His first jobs ended in failure. Intertwined through all of it was the drinking problem.

World War II was a four-year blur. The drinking problem was so bad after the war that he found himself on skid row. Now his logic is interesting. Dave had always said that he wasn't an alcoholic because alcoholics were skid-row bums. But here he was on skid row; therefore he was an alcoholic. I asked Dave about this and he said, "Hell, it never occurred to me that I was an alcoholic, because I knew I could pull myself out!" So goes the denial system. He enlisted in the Navy 1) because it represented a geographic cure, and 2) it got him off skid row.

Back as a civilian and in the jewelry business, Dave went the route of booze and women once more. His wife left him because of both. The job disintegrated again. What is alcoholism? It's trouble at home, at work, and in social life. But then, Dave wasn't an alcoholic, right? He took the geographic cure again; this time he traveled from Detroit to the Far West.

He arrived there with seventeen cents in his pocket; and within six years, he had parlayed that sum into ownership of two fairly large jewelry stores, which he promptly drank up. I believe that it would be safe to say that alcohol consumption was a source of trouble in his work life.

Bankruptcy is a sobering thought to many, but it was not so to Dave. It meant going to work for someone else again. His sideline business produced the real cash flow at this time. But it ended promptly with a suicide attempt. One hundred Librium tablets plus one fifth of Scotch was hardly a gesture.

Alcoholics are an extremely high-risk group for suicide. The practicing alcoholic has a definitely reduced future prospect. Many alcoholics are in a chronic state of hopelessness. Impulsive behavior is readily explained on this basis alone. An alcoholic operates in a fog. There's little rationality.

Many are involved in head-on auto collisions; many jump into crowds off buildings —

irrational acts which are committed in the fog of alcoholism. The suicides are not necessarily on the lower socioeconomic levels either. A study of the Journal of the American Medical Association's obituary pages indicated that five percent of the number of total deaths of physicians were suicides. Alcohol and drug abuse were observed in 40 percent of the cases.

Interestingly enough, alcoholism is found to be more prevalent among suicide attempts than among successful suicides. This makes sense, because the alcoholic is operating in such a fog that he is less likely to complete the job. Middle-aged white males are the prime candidates. A crisis is usually involved. Depression hangs heavily over the head. One study indicated that *25 percent* of suicides had been drinking just before death. Intoxication is even more associated with murders. Often the victims are inebriated.

Violence is usually associated with an alcoholic's suicide. Dave's attempt was nonviolent. Hanging, drowning, the use of sharp-edged tools — these are the usual methods. The extrovert is more likely to try it. Dave was definitely an extrovert.

Seventy-five percent of adult *overdosers* are women. The female favorites are Tuinal, Librium, Valium, Seconal, and straight Phenobarbital; alcohol, of course, is far and away the most abused depressant drug. The depression produced by alcohol causes people to reach for the pills. Sleeplessness is a favorite ploy here. The sleeplessness is usually the result of alcohol abuse. Pills are prescribed to help the alcoholic sleep; but so often they are used for suicide.

It is estimated that the suicide rate of alcoholics is 60 times that of the general populace. And there are 10 million alcoholic Americans! The figures are probably unrealistically low. Because of the stigma of the word "alcoholism," physicians attempt to protect the families. They simply leave the word "alcoholism" off the death certificate. For instance, it is likely that 98 percent of cirrhosis deaths are due to alcohol; death certificates will read "liver damage." Seldom is any mention made of alcohol on the death certificate. Pills are ever so much more respectable.

Now after Dave's suicide attempt, his physicians suggested changing occupations. Ludicrous! Dave had peddled papers, sold peanuts and popcorn, worked as a clerk, was a Navy corpsman, a jeweler, a jewelry salesman, an Army pharmacist's technician — and now he's told the answer to his problem is to change occupations! Anything but hanging the blame where it should be hung. Anything but telling him that it doesn't really make a difference what job he has because, as an *alcoholic,* he'll meet disaster. His problem all along was addiction to alcohol. People love to blame pressure for their drinking. "Get a job with less pressure." But life is pressure. What job doesn't have pressure?

Alcohol is bad news to the heart. Alcohol abuse contributes heavily to hypertension. Hypertension contributes to strokes and cardiovascular problems. Coronary problems seem to be the alcoholic's lot. Dave survived his first coronary. He left the hospital, and within a few weeks he was back for another five weeks, most of it in intensive care. He was drinking heavily very soon after he hit the hospital's exit door. His basic problem was alcoholism; the heart was secondary. When Dave left the hospital, he joined the ranks of thousands of other patients leaving hospitals that day with nothing done for their primary problem.

On his arrival home, he thought he'd be welcomed with open arms. It was not so. The way to handle that problem was obvious. Here he was just out of the hospital. He did what most alcoholics would do; he got even with his family by getting drunk — for three months. At the state's drying-out facility, for the first time in his life he began to think of himself as an alcoholic. Incredible, isn't it? His whole life was alcoholism. Like millions of others he was killing himself with alcohol. He was dying by inches and hadn't even the faintest idea of what was happening. He would be just as well off if he had cancer. His prognosis would probably be better.

We do see people like Dave who have survived skid row and made a real success of life. Alcoholics Anonymous Chapters are full of Daves — successful Daves. Dave isn't just living. He isn't just a man who no longer is a liability to society. He is a taxpayer. He contributes in a thousand ways to make life better for others.

Let me relate a little act of kindness that I happen to know about Dave. Remember, this was a man who up until three years before won prizes for being a champion TAKER. He was on his way back from a mining town where he had gone on business. As a seasoned traveler, he had rules he lived by. One of them was "never pick up a hitch-hiker." Outside this town stood three hitch-hikers — a man, woman, and child. He picked them up. Old hard-hearted Dave slammed on his brakes and picked them up. They had come from the East seeking work. Told that the mines were hiring, they hopped a bus and headed West. There was no work. They had no money. They had slept in the fields that night, and it was cold. Their little girl was under two years of age. Dave bought them lunch, and took them to a motel in the city. The next day he took them to an agency where they could get help. He paid all their bills. We *hear* quite a bit about the Good Samaritan, but I wonder how often we see a Good Samaritan in action.

Sure, Dave will be fighting his alcohol problem for the rest of his life. Until then, he will make hundreds of friends who will love him dearly, and will have an arm-length list of people who owe a lot to him. He's no longer a TAKER — now he's a GIVER. It shows in his face.

13

"I only drink on weekends."

The first time Sherry got drunk was when she was 15. She thought little of it. She had been drinking for several years, and it was "just one of those things that happens at parties." It happened again several times during her high school days, mostly at "beer busts."

Sherry got to know her real mother at age 21. She hadn't seen her for over 10 years. Her mother was a chronic addictive alcoholic. She drank from morning to night. Every day was an "alcoholiday." Sherry recalls being shocked by the amount of drinking *both* her mother and father did. Apparently about the only things her father fixed around the house were Manhattans and martinis. She vowed *never ever* to drink like that! The family she was raised with drank "moderately" — whatever that is.

Sherry drank conservatively up until she was about 27. She remembers getting loaded only once or twice during that entire time. At age 27, however, she forgot her "vow," so to speak, and started to drink regularly on the weekends and on her "days off." She found herself drinking to get drunk. She never regarded that as a significant problem, because it was only "weekends." She was at the controls. She didn't drink like her parents who drank every day; therefore, they were alcoholics. Her drinking was entirely different.

However, trouble began to creep into the picture. A weekend of drinking resulted in a pregnancy and a subsequent abortion. Because of her intoxicated state at the time, Sherry really never knew exactly what happened. Up until the age of 30, she steadfastly maintained that since her drinking was confined to weekends, no problem existed. Everyone she knew seemed to support that idea.

It was important to Sherry that she not be like her parents in their drinking habits. For three years she fought like a tigress to control her habit . . . no drinking during the week, no drinking even on Sundays. (Sundays were reserved to get over Saturday's hangover.) Oh, she admitted that she loved booze, but she was still different. She had control. Her drinking was not like that of her parents. So far, so good.

At about the age of 30, her control got a little shaky. She started drinking now and then during the week. But she caught herself; and through sheer will power she reverted to weekend drinking. She blamed her daily drinking on the trauma of the abortion. At any rate, she didn't allow her daily drinking to progress. Life had become a bit of a drag about that time anyway, so she moved on to greener pastures. She gave up a 13-year job to get away. (A "geographic cure" again?)

"Lost Wages," New Mexico, wasn't exactly a honeymoon for her. Her job lasted only four months. Drinking played a major role in the situation, but at the time she said she left because of "poor working conditions." She knocked around for several more months in Las Vegas, and ended up marrying a man she met in a bar. With typical alcoholic thinking, she reasoned that since they both had drinking problems, they would make a wonderful couple. Of course, it didn't work out.

After several months of torture, Sherry tried AA. She heard about it somewhere, and made the connection. She and her new husband marched off to an AA meeting hand in hand. The new husband enjoyed the meetings so much that he celebrated immediately after them. Looking back, Sherry says her husband had a wide range of moods: jocose, morose, bellicose, lachrymose, and comatose. She threw him out, ending nine months of marital bliss. AA didn't turn her on either, so she continued to drink heavily — not just on weekends. She drank all the time.

After months of continuous drinking, Sherry had the fortitude to pull herself back into line and go back to weekend boozing. She supported herself working as a barmaid. After about a year of being on this treadmill, she folded up her Las Vegas tent and went back home.

Once home, Sherry met another man in a bar, and remarried ... (sound familiar?). Wonder of all wonders, this man had a drinking problem too. We learn by experience, right? Before we get too critical, however, it helps to keep things in perspective. Sherry was half in the bag a good part of the time, and when you hang out in bars, the chances are fairly good that selection of a marriage partner will be somewhat limited. The marriage turned out to be another disaster.

But Sherry did try. She hauled her husband off to a marriage counselor. She wanted the marriage to work. After a trial separation of six weeks, they put it back together and took another stab at it. Their residence was a trailer. She went out one afternoon to visit her mother. Some time later, she received a phone call informing her that their trailer had burned to the ground, and that her husband had died in the fire. After she left for her visit he had hit the bottle; and fires have a strange way of starting when one is not in total control. She spent the next four months in an alcoholic blur.

Sherry reacted like an alcoholic pro. She didn't eat. The amount of alcohol she consumed approached the "self-destruct" level. She kept sinking lower and lower until she finally asked for help. She was ready for help.

During treatment, Sherry took a good look at her life. She saw quite clearly that most of her problems were the result of her drinking, not the other way around. She used alcohol to escape but eventually became the prisoner. Now she's heavily involved in AA, and she's beginning to look at life differently. She has taken a good look at herself too, and she knows she has a lot going for her. There is more to life than hurt and pain. Without booze to drag her down, she'll grow. It won't happen overnight, but the spark is there. Her chances of success are good.

There is a predominant theme in Sherry's story that's worth pondering. Specifically, it's "weekend drinking." Another interesting point is that both of her parents were alcoholics — so often we run into that circumstance. Sherry was disgusted with the continuous drinking of her parents. For years she hardly even took a drink because of this. That's reasonable conduct. It is common to see children avoiding alcohol like the plague because of unpleasant memories. They recall embarrassing and sometimes horrible cir-cumstances directly attributed to drunken-ness on the part of one or both parents. Children carry those memories vividly etched in their subconscious.

Theoretically, this results in what is called "generation gapping." Junior sees Dad crocked as often as he sees him sober. He sees Dad spend every dime he makes on booze. Junior himself has to work like a fool. The money he brings in often makes the difference between starvation and food on the table. He witnesses scenes of verbal and physical combat between his parents. His mother works her fingers to the bone, and as a reward she is shamelessly mistreated. To Junior, drinking becomes an *avoidance obsession.* He wouldn't take a drink under pain of death. It happens. The drinking pattern skips that generation, but the subsequent generation often gets hit broadside.

Apparently, Sherry was shaken badly by her real parents' drinking habits. As a backlash, aside from a few episodes as a high school girl, she drank very little until she reached her late twenties. When she did start drinking, it was primarily on weekends. "I'm not an alcoholic because I only drink on weekends." (So often, however, a drinker's weekend lasts from Friday to the following Wednesday.) As already noted, Sherry restricted her drinking to Saturdays — primarily because she needed all of Sunday to get over the effects of the "Irish virus" contracted the day before. Her childhood memories were like a drill sergeant shouting: "Get back in line!" Alcoholics drink all the time. "Normal" people reserve their drinking for weekends! Sure they do!

It is interesting to note the pattern of progression in almost every alcoholic's drinking history. Looking back over Sherry's life, it is easy to see the handwriting on the wall. It always is. Monday morning quarterbacking of alcoholics is a pleasure, unless you happen to be the losing quarterback. Anyone can predict the inexorable fall. Sheer will power confined

Sherry's drinking to weekends. Eventually she lost. Perhaps it was the crisis of the horrible abortion. One cannot help thinking that if it had not been that crisis, it would have been another.

Alcoholism is a *progressive disease*. It just keeps getting steadily worse. The alcoholic may pick up a yard here and there, but will lose two before you know it. There'll always be those periods of sobriety where things begin to look up; but they never last long, unless, of course, lightning strikes. Until then, looking over the alcoholic's drinking history is like following the descent of a mountain climber. This is hardly news for alcoholics. Most of them worth their salt can trace their ruination step by step without difficulty.

Another interesting point in this story is the "big move." It is remarkable how many alcoholics do this. That "big move" solves all . . . new faces, new friends, but the same old drinking problem remains. It solved nothing in Sherry's life. She gave up a job she had held for 13 years to make her move. Instead of solving her problem, it only complicated it. That seems to be a pattern also.

I wonder how many "Sherrys" harbor the misconception that because they are able to restrict their drinking to certain periods, they do not have a problem. I wonder how many of them ever sit down and speculate why they bother at all to make a point of limiting their drinking to weekends. If drinking is no problem, why limit it? Ninety million Americans are able to take it or leave it. They don't have to play such games. They are able to take those few drinks and walk away. Alcoholics simply do not do that. Sherry knew she had a problem. Her parents sowed the seeds. She knew. She fought the good fight, but she lost. But look at the bruises — two tragic marriages, jobs lost, misery, money problems. That's quite a lot for a little girl to haul around.

I suspect there are many persons, both male and female, who relate strongly to Sherry's history. Right now, she's a pretty little girl with a solid foot on the road to sobriety. She's lucky. Those other "weekenders" aren't so lucky. They'll progress, just as she did. They'll go from short weekends to longer weekends, to continuous drinking, to abstinence or to death.

14

"I drink because I can't sleep."

There is no worse drug than alcohol for the relief of sleeplessness. Alcohol is metabolized roughly at the rate of one drink per hour; therefore, the nervous system is jangled as if by a four-alarm fire after only a few hours of sleep. Granted, enough booze may cause you to go to sleep (and perhaps into a permanent coma), but as soon as that blood alcohol level is gone, there's that heavy price that must be paid. The dues are rather stiff.

Question. Why are heavy drinkers always tired? Because they don't know what good sound sleep is. Alcohol helps people sleep, right? Wrong! Present findings indicate that alcohol actually causes insomnia. Insomnia, if it is bad enough, could cause a "social drinker" to hit the juice so hard that the "line" could be crossed, and the so-called "social drinker" could become an alcoholic. It all gets to be a wee bit confusing. You can't sleep, so you drink. The drink causes insomnia; the insomnia causes you to drink more, and the more you drink the more likely it is that you will become an alcoholic. This sounds a little like the old ditty: "The more you study the more you forget; the more you forget the less you know; the less you know the dumber you get . . . so why study?"

The sleep of alcoholics differs from that of nonalcoholics. Their sleep is characterized by many nighttime awakenings and low total sleep time. Alcoholics have lower than normal deep and dreaming sleep. Through the use of sleep laboratories we have learned that normal people go through sleep stages. The transition from stage to stage is ordinarily smooth. All of this has been documented by brain-wave studies called electroencephalo-grams. Alcoholics have a high frequency of shifting from stage to stage. Their patterns resemble "Ping-Pong ball" fluctuations.

Alcoholics aren't the only ones who suffer sleep disturbances. Abusers of opiates and amphetamines, as well as almost all the sleeping pills, fall into this category of sleep disturbance. Alcoholics are famous (infamous is a better term) for abusing all sedative drugs, particularly sleeping pills. The build-up of tolerance to those pills is quick, and routine doses soon become a bit of a joke. And this all adds up. Those who drink anything from a pint on up (or one and one-half six-packs of beer) are drinking the equivalent of several sleeping pills. This goes on for years and years. Imagine what happens when a physi-cian gives such persons a couple of puny sleeping pills. They're only a drop in the ocean. But when alcohol is mixed with the pills, a dangerously serious predicament arises.

Many famous men and women have died from the combination of sleeping pills and booze. It would take several pages to list their names. Hundreds of thousands of not-so-famous people have destroyed themselves too, either by planned suicide or by accidental death.

The problem with giving alcoholics sleeping pills is obvious. Practicing alcoholics aren't going to take one pill to go to sleep! Half an hour after they take a few of the pills, they'll not remember whether they took any of them at all. When persons are crocked they simply do not know what they are doing. This is a guaranteed way to rub out alcoholics. Yet, so often alcoholics can walk into a physician's office, and a great percentage of the time all they have to do is ask for sleeping pills and they'll be readily prescribed.

Drugs are fascinating. Most people are familiar with "speed." It is used in great quantities by "fat burners," that is, by physicians who specialize in weight reduction. It is also big on the street. People love the way it "speeds" up the system — hence, the name. It makes the mind perk up, causes everything to shift gears upward — all live action. People use it to stay awake also. Chronic ingestion of this stimulant may lead to insomnia. The more you take, the higher the tolerance. To some people the drug becomes so mind-altering that they actually *cannot* sleep without it.

Insane as it sounds, the system adjusts so that people have to ingest a drug that ordinarily keeps them awake in order to go to sleep. However, as the liver "learns" to metabolize the drug, the patient "runs out" of medication, like a car running out of gas, in the middle of the night — hence, insomnia.

Sleep laboratories have taught us a lot about sleep and sleeping pills. When patients (alcoholic or nonalcoholic) take pills for sleep, the actual effect wears off in a few weeks. That's right — after a few weeks that pill works about as well as a placebo (a sugar pill). What do the patients do? They take more. Even after larger doses, they do not sleep well. That's a fact — a fact that many people do not want to hear. It is almost humorous to see the spouse of an alcoholic breathing fire about liquor, when at the same time he/she refuses to accept the plain fact about that little sleeping pill in the medicine cabinet. "Now, you're meddling" is the usual answer here.

The most important thing to understand is that alcohol *by itself,* in large enough quantities, can kill. It can depress the central nervous system so that the respiratory system is knocked out. Sleeping pills do the same thing. And both together form a lethal combination.

The person, then, who drinks to go to sleep is way off base. Alcohol is metabolized quickly, and one thing the nervous system does not need is a two a.m. New Year's Eve party. Alcoholics are notoriously poor sleepers. They go to bed tired, they get up tired. REM (rapid eye movement) sleep is critical for proper rest. Twenty-five percent of the good sleep is REM sleep. Alcohol robs the alcoholic of REM sleep. This has been well documented in sleep laboratories More importantly, it may be a year before normal sleep is restored after the alcoholic is off the sauce.

There are practical measures to help the alcoholic through this period of sleep deprivation. The best antidote is exercise. Jogging, playing tennis, biking, dancing, javelin throwing, digging ditches — anything at all that sends you to bed in a state of physical exhaustion. The exercise should not be performed just before retiring; it "revs" up the motor too much. Also, soaking in a hot tub for 10 minutes before going to bed is a great relaxant.

Of course, the best help of all for the alcoholic is attendance at AA meetings. A placid mind will quickly drop off into the arms of Morpheus. Problems on the mind make it difficult to sleep. A placid mind and a tired body are a winning combination.

Biofeedback and meditation are two new areas that seem to be of great benefit to the recovering alcoholic in reestablishing good sleep patterns. Both of these therapeutic methods restore peace to ravaged nervous systems. They can work miracles for those who are willing to work themselves. Like anything worthwhile, interest, practice, and diligence are required. If mastered, they may become a real boon.

The last thing the alcoholic needs is another drug habit. The sleeping pill habit should be avoided like the plague. *One* pill is bad. The alcoholic will end up abusing pills just like he or she abused ethanol. All mind-altering drugs must be avoided if the alcoholic intends to survive. Half measures only lead back to the bottle.

15
"I just go on a bender now and then."

There are such things as "periodic alcoholics," that is, those who go on drinking binges. They may drink socially for years and years with no trouble. They then start to go on "binges" or "drunks." These last for a few days or a few weeks at a time. The binges eventually get closer together and they last longer and longer. Eventually the "periodic alcoholic" goes down the tubes with about as much grace and elegance as any other drunk.

In some ways, "periodic alcoholics" have a much worse prognosis than those who are "hammered" all the time. Those who drink all the time *know* they're in trouble. Tell them they've got to lay off the booze and they'll laugh, because they've known that for years. They either 1) haven't the guts to quit, or 2) their brains are too far gone, or 3) they're too lazy to do anything about it. Telling chronic addictive alcoholics to quit drinking is like telling them they should give up breathing. The man or woman who is a chronic addictive alcoholic is always in trouble.

Why should "periodic alcoholics" ask for help? As far as they are concerned, they don't and never did have the remotest problem. They can stop whenever they want. In fact, they stop for months at a time. But during that period much of their thinking is about their next drinking spree. And they may spend $5,000 in one spree. Meanwhile, their binges keep getting closer and closer together. Their main trouble is that they are too stubborn to listen to reason.

Let me tell you about a friend of mine. Phil is a gentleman. He was educated at one of the finest engineering schools in the country. His relatives were proud and prosperous. One uncle was a United States Senator, but as Phil says, "You can't hold that against him." Phil wasn't a world class athlete, but he was good enough to qualify for the Olympic swimming team. He was no slouch any way you cut it.

Phil liked to drink, but it was no problem. It seldom is in the beginning. He worked as an engineer for several years, being employed by a large steel company. Part of his job consisted of entertaining. He could drink just about all his companions under the table, and still drive them home. Sound familiar? It was a macho thing and he was a macho guy.

In 1927 he was sent to Russia to put up a steel mill. What he remembered most about this first trip was that the Communist Party assigned a woman to keep an eye on him the whole time he was there. He didn't mind that so much, but she was six feet four inches tall, and had a nose to match her height. She was into his books, letters, and drawings. Angry at her tactics, he was tempted to stand on a chair and pound her into the floor. Unfortunately, however, she outweighed him by 100 pounds!

After that first trip, his company sent him back to put up a second steel mill in Russia. The job took a couple of years. He finished that job in 1933. The next six years he represented his company in Europe, floating mostly between Paris and London. His drinking became more constant, particularly during the day. He began drinking his lunch. As he traveled all over Europe, he became more dependent on alcohol, but it did not bother him. When the war broke out, Phil went back to the States and found himself building a magnesium plant outside one of our Southwestern cities. For the first time, his drinking really got in the way. Rather than be fired, he gracefully joined the Navy. He was 40 years old at the time.

Phil spent four years in the Seabees. He never let his duty interfere with his drinking. He considered himself a "periodic type" drinker, but refused to consider it a problem. A leave meant a binge. And the binges kept getting closer and closer together.

After the war, Phil started his own company. He prospered. In two years, he started another company — working out patents for chemical plants. He made a pile of money and drank more booze. By 1961, it all got a little too much, so he sold his companies and moved to

Mexico. Three years later, his nondrinking wife divorced him and took him for a large portion of his fortune. This didn't help his drinking or his disposition.

Phil first heard of AA in 1951. He remembers telling an AA member that if he ever developed a drinking problem, he'd let him know. Eight months later and several thousand dollars poorer, he decided he might have a drinking problem. He became involved in AA — which is to say that he went to a lot of meetings. He had a period of 36 months of sobriety, another of 23 months, and another one of 18 months. He'd go to meetings and give all the right answers; but AA principles remained in his head, never reaching his gut. The periods of sobriety became less and less.

Phil was a voracious reader. He read every alcoholism journal published. As a scientist, he felt that sooner or later a chemical would be discovered which would solve his alcohol problem. Unfortunately, scientists are still looking for said chemical.

He took Antabuse even before it became available in the States; he had it smuggled in from Canada. He stayed sober for a while on it. It can be said that he tried everything.

In 1967, he found himself in a halfway house. The place was so bad he could barely stand its stench, but he sobered up for the umpteenth time. Two things happened after that. He married a good woman and he got religion. He's been sober over 10 years now.

Phil married an alcoholic. A lovelier woman you'd never want to meet — a real lady in the full sense of the word. Together they made two plus two equal five. They had been college sweethearts; but both had gone their separate ways, only to find each other again many years later. Interestingly, Phil did not know that she had a history of alcoholism when they were married. They've made it together.

Phil got "religion," but not in the sense that we ordinarily use the term. For the first time in his life, he honestly took the *First Step* in AA. The First Step goes like this: "We admitted that we were powerless over alcohol — that our lives had become unmanageable." That's a giant step for a proud man like Phil. He had spent the better part of 16 years in AA, mouthing this step, and *never* did he really get into it.

"Powerless" and *"unmanageable"* connote *defeat.* Phil defeated? Impossible! He'd built steel factories; managed two big companies. He'd hobnobbed with moneyed people and leaders everywhere. He'd come from a fine, well-known family. Phil defeated? He certainly was — landed flat on his back. Like most proud men and women, it was a tremendous blow to his ego. The bigger the ego, the harder it is to admit defeat. *Achievers* often never make, or take, that First Step.

Phil spent 16 years playing, *"Yes, but." "Yes, but* if it wasn't for that woman I married." *"Yes, but,* if it wasn't for my anxiety." *"Yes, but* if it wasn't for that rotten break." *"Yes, but* if it

wasn't for the situation in Outer Mongolia."
"Yes, but . . . ," "Yes, but . . . ," "Yes, but . . ."
— favorite words of those with monumental
egos.

"Powerless" is a ponderous word. "Here I
am!" "I'm nothing!" "I'm a punching bag!"
Picture a successful engineer, a successful
physician, a successful professor, a successful lawyer, a successful clergyman admitting
that he's powerless. It takes a big person to
admit that.

"Powerless" also connotes loss of control.
And that's hard for achievers to take. They are
"do as I say" people. "MY WILL BE DONE!" All
of a sudden, they have to admit a drug —
alcohol — has gotten the upper hand. They
are powerless over it. They have lost control.
Alcohol now controls. They've lost. Phil lost
and he admitted it for the very first time. He
had paid lip service to AA for years, but in 1967
he knew he had had it, and honestly admitted
it.

I wonder how many people have touched
but the periphery of AA without really getting
into it. Every time I hear the phrase "I tried AA
but it wasn't for me," I think of an entire
segment of so-called AA members who have
never gotten past this First Step. They give the
others a bad name. All you can say about them
is that at least they're trying — not making it,
but at least trying.

The First Step is quite an achievement all by
itself. Phil finally joined the winners. He claims
to this day that the forces in his life that made

the difference were: 1) the love and respect of a good woman, and 2) understanding and honestly taking the First Step in AA. It sounds so easy, but it turns out to be so difficult.

Phil's religion is hardly what you would call "organized." His moral code is quite strict. He rigidly maintains that those who mouth the tenets of Christianity but do not practice them are hypocrites, and they'll never accept AA. Although he is not well, he spends a major portion of his day helping others. Often he acts as an AA sponsor. He's no longer loaded with money, but he is extremely generous with what he has left. He and his wife still make two or three AA meetings a week. His life is full. When he dies, he probably won't be canonized, but he'll be up there with the saints — probably asking where the closest AA meeting is. Yes, he has religion. He's also one of my best friends. I probably shouldn't be allowed in the same room with him.

"Periodic alcoholics" — the world is full of them. Practically all of them have a few things in common: (1) they don't think they have a drinking problem; (2) through the years, their "binges" get closer together; (3) their prognosis is very bad, probably worse than the continuous drinker; and (4) they are directly responsible for much of the tragedy associated with alcoholism.

These are the people who abstain for months at a time but always manage to botch it. They are accidents waiting to happen. They continue to hope for some crisis to develop which will give them an excuse for drinking. If one doesn't come along conveniently, they'll create one. And when they drink, they really drink — auto accidents, murders in blackouts, manslaughter, loss of lifetime savings, quickie marriages and quickie divorces. Their favorite cry after all the trouble they've caused: "It'll never happen again!" "I've learned my lesson!" "I've stopped before, and I can do it again!" And they will play this tune until they die — or, like Phil, they decide to quit playing games and *do* something other than talk about it. It's work, but the rewards are there. You see "Phils" at many an AA meeting.

I ran across a beautiful message the other day. The author is apparently unknown. It went like this:

God in his wisdom selected this group of men and women to be the purveyors of his goodness. In selecting those who were to do this work, he went not to the proud and mighty, the famous or the brilliant. He went instead to the humble, to the sick, to the unfortunate. He went right to the drunkard; the so-called weakling of the world.

Well might he have said: Into your weak and feeble hands, I have assigned a power beyond estimate. To you has been given that which has been denied the learned of your fellows. Not to scientists or statesmen, nor to wives or mothers, not even to my priests or ministers have I given this gift of healing other alcoholics which I entrust to you.

It must be used unselfishly; it carries with it grave responsibility. No day can be too long, no demands on your time can be too urgent, no case too pitiful, no task too hard, no effort too great. It must be used with tolerance, for I have restricted its use to no race, no creed, no one denomination.

Personal criticism you must expect; lack of appreciation will be common, ridicule will be your lot, your motives will be misjudged. You must be prepared for adversity, for what man calls adversity is the ladder you must use to ascend the rungs toward spiritual perfection. And remember, in the exercise of this power, I shall not exact from you beyond your capabilities. You are not selected because of your exceptional talents. Be careful always — if success attends your efforts — not to ascribe to personal superiority that to which you can lay claim only by virtue of my gift.

If I had wanted learned men to accomplish this mission, the power would have been entrusted to the physician and scientist. If I had wanted eloquent men, there would have been many anxious for the assignment, for talk is the easiest use of all talents with which I have endowed mankind. If I had wanted scholarly men, the world is filled with better qualified men than you who would be available. You were selected because you have been the outcasts of the world, and your long experience as drunkards has made, or should make, you humbly alert to the cries of distress that come from the lonely hearts of alcoholics everywhere.

Keep in mind the admission you made on the day of your profession in AA, namely, that you are powerless and that it was only with your willingness to turn your life and will unto my keeping that relief came to you.

Quite an epistle!

16

"I only drink socially."

Ann sat at her breakfast table one morning, sipping stale wine and thinking about her situation. Her hands were trembling. She had just witnessed her husband go off to work with slumped shoulders and obvious depression. Her beautiful daughter had told her the night before that she hated her. And she had overheard the same daughter calling her sister long distance and advising her not to come "this summer." For the first time in her life, she faced the fact that she was an alcoholic. She arose from the table, went over to the sink and poured the wine down the drain. She picked up the phone and called Alcoholics Anonymous. That was two weeks ago.

Ann looks at alcohol like she would a person. When she was introduced to alcohol in college it became an immediate "friend." After marrying an Army officer, she came to accept alcohol as a charming prelude to a dinner party, or a relaxing evening of dancing, card playing, etc. (No problem.)

They were transferred to Berlin. There they found that liquor was cheap and entertainment was inexpensive. Maid service was free, and the homes were large and often luxurious. Those happy days were filled with fond memories plus booze of all kinds — champagne, Scotch, bourbon, leisurely sipped cocktails and highballs.

They spent a year in Munich. Ann learned to appreciate the great German beer. She recalls with pleasure all the magnificent scenery and wonderful times she and her growing family enjoyed. She also remembers that all those good times were had with drink in hand. (Still no problem.)

Ann and her husband stayed in the Army. He was a successful career officer; she a successful Army wife. They raised three children while moving frequently. Ann actively filled the role of military mother and wife. As the children matured, it left more freedom for them to socialize. Socialize they did. The question most often asked during this period was: "What'll it be?"

Another trip to Europe ended with Ann and the booze getting to be inseparable companions. Rhine wines became her favorites. Her trips throughout the Continent became more and more involved with drinking. (The line was coming into view.)

But, like all endeavors, not all military jobs and military moves are beds of roses. Ann's husband got locked into a position that put him under exceptional pressure. The ever-willing helpmate met him at the door with a pitcher of "you know whats" every night. She could hardly be expected not to share in the unwinding process, and it became a ritual. The Base boasted cheap help in the home. There was no television, radio, or telephone, but an awful lot of leisure. The drinking got serious. She became jealous of anything that interfered with her drinking time. (No longer nebulous, the line came into full view.)

Ann slipped across the line of alcoholism ever so effortlessly. The changes were subtle. She didn't laugh much any more. She didn't dance much any more. She became more and more dependent on her drinking. Physically sick, she found herself doing things she never would have dreamed of doing years before. She said things she loathed. Mentally depressed, she lost command of herself. Alcohol was now in control.

Her family began to hate the very presence of ethanol. Her children came to visit her less, and they left sooner. Ann began to experience blackouts. She came to know terror, clammy sweats, hysteria, tears, scars, and festering physical and mental wounds. In short, she entered the wonderful, enjoyable, hilarious life of the typical female alcoholic.

Ann's life as a practicing alcoholic hopefully ended with her call to AA. She was directed to our treatment center. With God's help, with Ann's help, with AA's help, she will be a winner. After just two weeks, she has fallen in love with AA. She has some of the old sparkle back in her face. She is getting her act together quickly. Will she make it? Only time will tell. Ann is just like everyone else. She'll make it if she works very hard in AA. If she attends several meetings a week for the next few years and if she keeps a clear head and an open mind, she'll make it. She'll live the next 30 years as a "giver" instead of a "taker."

Ann's story is not all that unusual. She can probably name 10 close friends who are as bad as she was with their drinking. Military wives are prone to alcoholism. Military life gravitates to alcoholism. It is a life conducive to drinking, and the military are by nature the macho of all macho groups. The men are expected to be boozers. I've never been able to understand why, but they are.

We tend to forget that military wives have problems similar to their husbands'. They attend the same parties, suffer the same agonies of promotion and demotion, and fight the same battles as corporate wives. They stand the same chance of becoming addicted to alcohol. And when booze dominates, disaster strikes.

Female alcoholics are not viewed in the same way as male alcoholics. The female is expected to drink and be merry, but she must not go over the line. The husband develops alcoholism, and everyone says "too bad." The wife develops alcoholism, and everyone says "it's a disgrace." For some reason, ladies are supposed to develop a magic immunity. It doesn't happen. It certainly didn't happen to Ann.

From 1972 to 1976, the service allocated about 57 million dollars for alcohol control problems. For years we heard the cry: "Save the serviceman from heroin! Save the serviceman from pot!" But the most prevalent drug abused by those in service is now and probably always will be alcohol. The Department of Defense is acutely aware of its severe alcohol problem.

Military service is hierarchical, paternalistic, and permissive of alcohol abuse. It is also highly mobile and male-dominated. In these respects it is somewhat different from the civilian populace. Alcohol is cheap, particularly on the Base. The mobility factor is a built-in geographic change. "My next assignment will get me away from the boozers on this post. With a change of friends, a change of jobs, and relief of pressure, there is bound to be less drinking." Sure! Only thing is when you're an alcoholic, things seldom get better, they get progressively worse. A change of climate, a change of locale, a change of faces — these only present the same problem. They certainly didn't help Ann much.

One advantage of being alcoholics in the service is the control over patient referral, length of stay in the hospital, and a regular clinical review of patients. The drawback is that what happens in industry also happens here. People get kicked upstairs: a true example of the Peter Principle. The buddy system prevails. Cover, cover, cover . . . until it is too late. Wait until they are basket cases, then boot them out. Never mention alcohol, never mention treatment; wait until they get so close to the edge that a feather is sufficient to make them fall over.

Rank, as usual, doesn't seem to make all that much difference. As in industry, the people at the top readily point the finger at the troops below, but the fickle finger is often shaky. As in industry, mistakes at the top from the boozer are just more costly. The price is dearly paid, up and down the ranks.

The wives of servicemen pay the *same* price. God help the wife who turns out to be a boozer! In the closet she goes. Don't let anyone know Ann's got a problem — that'll be the end of promotions. So, forget about Ann; it's the promotions that count. Keeping the secret carefully guarded guarantees that Ann will get no help.

One myth that dies a hard, slow death is that treatment is a waste of time. A recently reported study involved some 563 Navy and Marine enlisted men (between ages 18 and 47) who have been through rehabilitation centers. A 2-year follow-up at 6, 12, and 24-month intervals indicated that 83 percent of the subjects were considered effective by their commanding officers. That's not bad. I know of no such study involving military wives, but I imagine it would be at least comparable.

A program developed by the Navy recently reported similar progress. A 36-hour remedial education alcoholism program was completed on off-duty time. It consisted of screening, classwork training, instructor training, and civilian-military workshops. Two hundred sixty-seven members completed the course. Less than five percent have experienced difficulty with alcohol since. The total cost of the program was $155 per person. One good stiff weekend of drinking runs that much. So, some progress is being made.

The drinking housewife is sometimes called the "nine-to-three alcoholic." Female drinkers are different from male alcoholics in that they start later than men, and it takes them *less* time to cross the line. Many become confirmed alcoholics with just a few years of heavy drinking. Ann drank socially for the better part of 20 years. When she started to hit it heavy, it did not take very long to lose complete control.

Since there are no hard and fast rules on alcoholism, it is difficult to describe a typical drinking housewife. When this is done, we all have the tendency to look over a group of characteristics and say: "Well, that lets me out! I don't have any of those." For years people have tried to describe what a "typical female alcoholic housewife" is like. Here are my ideas on the subject.

1. She begins later (in her late forties) than a man, and has been an alcoholic probably eight years before seeking treatment.
2. She's married to an alcoholic (thirty-three percent chance) and has two children.

3. She blames her drinking on "depression."
4. Her father probably was an alcoholic.
5. She wants no one to know she's an alcoholic. She thinks that she has covered her tracks so well that even her husband doesn't even suspect. (More often than not, she's about the only one she has fooled.)
6. She avoids medical care because of fear of discovery.
7. She drinks alone and at home.
8. Her family helps keep her alcoholism a secret.
9. She drinks to relieve boredom, loneliness, and frustration.
10. She has average intelligence.
11. She has liver damage.

Ann's job of covering up was worthy of the CIA. But the enormous energy expended in trying to keep her drinking secret went for naught. Women finally recognize the spiritual beating they give themselves by putting up a front. Sooner or later the facade crumbles, and the emerging figure is one of abject defeat.

Often, pills are a problem at this stage. Sometimes they are used in an effort to end it all. Seventy-five percent of adult overdosers are women. Tuinol, Librium, Valium, and Phenobarbital seem to be their favorite pills. Women prefer to go out in style, with no pain if at all possible. They dress in their best and tend to make a production of it. About one in twenty-six completes the act. Many of their suicide gestures are thwarted by last-minute intervention. About one in four men who attempt suicide in this manner actually completes the act.

Alcohol is *very often* combined with pills. It may be the leading cause of accidental overdose. About 70 percent of men and 40 percent of women are drinking just before overdose. People generally do not have any idea how lethal the combination of alcohol and pills can be. Many never get a second chance to learn.

Women are more likely to get into a cross-addiction with alcohol and pills. Many physicians simply do not understand the significant danger of this problem. In difficult times, women are more likely to reach for a chemical crutch. Like ethanol, tranquilizers, sleeping pills, painkillers cure absolutely nothing. Amazing as it may seem, husbands often encourage their wives to drink. Reality sometimes is harsh to face. If half the effort exerted by many women in the area of secret drinking were expended in working at their sobriety — particularly in AA — there would be many more success stories. Still, adding it all up, I think that a woman's chance of achieving sobriety and keeping it is equal to if not better than that of a man. Maybe women have the edge in guts?

Some sources believe that the husband plays more of a significant role in the successful recovery of the wife than she does of an alcoholic husband. We have certainly witnessed such conduct in our facility. Rehabilitation needs support. Wives do ask their husbands for help. Husbands, on the contrary, are usually too proud to do so. Witness, for example, how reluctant men are to ask directions even when they are completely lost.

Like men, women go through a period of strain when middle age strikes. The middle-age mother whose children have matured is vulnerable to alcoholism. Her critical role in the family makes it imperative that the problem be faced immediately. It may be distasteful for the family members, but they'd better get with it. The "let the other guy do it" philosophy plays right into the hands of the alcoholic. Premenstrual drinking may be a clue to a future problem. If stress and tension are met with booze, one does not have to boast an IQ of 160 to figure the consequences.

It is my opinion that few alcoholics achieve good sobriety without Alcoholics Anonymous. I see very few men or women who attain long-term sobriety without it. I see many men and women who keep up a running fight with AA, and they are consistent losers. When most people want to win, they run with winners. Losers attract losers. Winners attract winners. AA is full of winners, long-term winners. The ranks of the losers are filled with people who "can't stand" AA. This has been my personal observation over a period of 10 years.

I think women have a greater need for AA than men do. Shedding the guilt of alcoholism is worse for women. Association with AA helps dispel that guilt. The admission of total defeat and inability to control drinking is very often equivalent to lifting an enormously depressing weight off tired shoulders. The peace and serenity that AA brings to the tortured soul of the alcoholic is something to behold.

The husband has an important role to play in the recovery of the alcoholic wife. Many men are completely unaware that an organization exists for husbands of alcoholics. It is called Male Al-Anon. When Al-Anon is discussed, many jump to the conclusion that it's strictly for women. Some of the very best men I know are members of Male Al-Anon groups.

Usually, it is quite difficult for a man to admit that his wife is an alcoholic. He may concede that she drinks too much, but he finds it hard to face the fact that she is an alcoholic. But when that happens, his role becomes a trying one. As one man explained to a group: "When you can come home some night and find your wife dead drunk on the front lawn and can step calmly over her (after placing a brick under her head so she won't drown when the sprinklers come on), go in the house, have a good meal, and get a good night's sleep — then, and then only, do you have it made in Al-Anon." One gets the picture.

Ann typifies the female alcoholic: upper middle class, married, mother of two, above-average intelligence, heavy into the drinking by her late forties, a secret drinker, protected by her family. It took her about four years to get wiped out. Her environment happened to be a great breeding ground for alcoholism. Will she make it? I think she will. She finished her treatment today and left in high spirits. Why will she make it? The best thing going for her is a positive, healthy attitude about AA. Social drinking is a dead issue. It had better be.

17

"I always eat when I drink."

Many people labor under the misconception that by mixing alcohol with food, the food provides some sort of magical cloak that prevents alcoholism. Wrong! All the food does is slow down the absorption of the alcohol. It therefore takes longer to get plastered. Of course, alcohol on an empty stomach is bad unless the intent is to get crocked in a hurry. Mixing the alcohol with ice, sugar, orange juice, lemon juice, etc. — all of these things help slow down the absorption.

Whether alcohol is taken straight or mixed with 100 other substances, it is either vomited or pulled out of the small intestine. It is then taken to the liver and metabolized there. A very small amount of alcohol is absorbed in the stomach; about 90 percent is absorbed in the 20 feet or so of the small intestine that we simply can't do without. It sounds all so simple and yet it is all so complicated.

One of the major wounds ethanol inflicts on the stomach is the damage it does to the gastric mucosa. The mucosa is the lining of the stomach. There's a natural barrier that protects that lining. Alcohol destroys that. Alcohol causes irritation of the cells that produce hydrochloric acid. Hydrochloric acid is necessary to produce acidity so we can digest food in the small gut. Alcohol causes overproduction of the acid. Overproduction of the acid causes ulcers, pain, and bleeding. A good percent of alcoholics have already undergone surgery for stomach problems before they get into treatment.

The routine story goes like this: Joe starts out with a good stomach. It has to be good or it would never take the abuse that Joe is about to heap upon it. Joe learns to drink booze — beer, gin, bourbon, Scotch, vodka. Because he has a good stomach, he gets away with it for a long time. His buddies drink the same amount and are vomiting halfway across the street. Joe becomes a legend because of the quantity he can drink and keep down. Joe continues to abuse his wonderful stomach. He becomes addicted to alcohol in the process, and the process escalates with the abuse. That wonderful stomach is no longer wonderful. After a time Joe is a regular in the physician's office. "See, Doc, it's this spicy food I've been eating!" — Like hell!

Very few heavy drinkers do not smoke. Smoking contributes to the acidity problem. Joe carries Tums, Rolaids, Gelusil, Mylanta, Maalox, Riopan, etc., to put out the perennial fire. Eventually bleeding starts. Three hospitalizations, $25,000 in medical bills, and at least one surgery later, someone mentions that Joe might be an alcoholic. So, they get him into treatment. If someone had gotten to Joe five years before, all of that might have been prevented.

It has been widely accepted that alcoholic beverages contain only *empty* calories. That means they lack minerals, vitamins, protein, etc. Alcohol *does* have calories, and generally they are marshalled quickly into fat. Many a martini drinker has been waltzing through life knocking down two or three before lunch, thinking that the lunch which follows covers him or her from the damage to the organs, particularly the liver. We now know that this is false security. The damage shows up anyway. This was recently demonstrated quite effectively in a New York study.

A group of volunteers were fed a good diet along with 6 drinks a day — a total of 10 ounces of 86-proof whiskey for 18 days. All of them exhibited clear evidence of liver changes after only a few days. None of them showed any *clinical* evidence of liver trouble. This means that there is liver damage, but the people never realize it.

Long-term studies made on 16 baboons were even more dramatic. All of them developed fatty livers after a short time. Five developed hepatitis. Six developed cirrhosis after two to four years. A control group getting the same diet, but *no alcohol,* showed no liver change.

Alcohol cannot be stored as such in the body. It is processed immediately by the liver, where the necessary enzymes are available. It is purely academic whether a person is an alcoholic or not in this matter. It is strictly a question of how much alcohol one drinks. Six beers, six highballs, six martinis, six shots — liver changes show up after a few days, regardless of whether the person eats or not.

In 1974, cirrhosis of the liver became the seventh-ranking cause of death among Americans. It outranks influenza and pneumonia. In urban areas, it ranks *third* as a cause of death.

An alcoholic's idea of a balanced diet is a drink in both hands. For many decades we have blamed poor health on the *lack of nutrition.* It is somewhat of a shock to learn that booze is the offending agent. But it would be wrong to assume that nutrition plays no role in this area. Nutrition seldom plays a minor role in any health process. Good food is essential to the health of any person, regardless of the disease. Diet should never be underestimated in its value to help the body recuperate. It is often much more important than any of our high-powered medications.

Vitamins have always played a major role in the treatment of the alcoholic. Alcoholics with malnutrition frequently suffer from vitamin deficiency. This is particularly true of the B vitamins. The two clinical effects of such a deficiency become evident in the form of peripheral neuropathy and mental changes.

Mental changes are often subtle. Memory loss, mood swings, irascibility, irrationality are just a few of the signs and symptoms noted. Peripheral neuropathy shows up in the form of loss of feeling in the extremities, loss of muscle strength, coordination failures, a different walking gait, etc. The changes can be subtle or profound.

Neither of these conditions is uncommon among heavy drinkers. Thiamine, riboflavin, nicotinic acid, pantothenic acid, folate are usually low both in the blood and the cerebrospinal fluid. B_{12} deficiency is very rare. A good general diet is usually all that is needed to correct these Vitamin B deficiencies, but we usually shotgun our patients with vitamins, just to play it safe.

A fact that we forget sometimes is that while the drinker is living on his alcohol, the body is losing amino acids, potassium, magnesium, zinc, and vitamins. These must be replaced or a deficit results. Since ethanol is "empty" of calories, these must be pulled from reserves. Even though we now know that the liver is worked to a frazzle detoxifying alcohol, we also know that the essential elements are being used up and are not being replaced. This is bound to be a factor in the situation.

Some people believe that vitamins increase the oxidation of alcohol. Take vitamins, they say, and the blood alcohol goes down. That's not true. But taking vitamins along with booze — if one must — does help cover the deficit.

Polyneuropathy and myopathy are terms many alcoholics become familiar with sooner or later. Polyneuropathy is a general term which is characterized by tingling and numbness of the hands and feet. Sensation may be lost altogether. Pain may be present, particularly at night. *Myopathy* results in weakness and pain in the extremities. It is probably due to the direct effect of alcohol on the individual organelles inside the muscle cells. Muscle pathology may also result from diarrhea. Anyone who has ever contracted Montezuma's revenge knows how a few days' persistent diarrhea leaves every muscle hurting. Pity the chronic alcoholic whose gut is worn out most of the time. Many die from diarrhea. Their muscles simply waste away.

The controversy over what causes the liver pathology in heavy drinkers has been fairly well documented. Nutritional deficits are still in the running, but the direct effect of alcohol as a toxic substance has jumped in the lead without question. Heavy drinkers are dying daily from liver pathology, regardless of the cause; and the most pathetic point about this is that so many are dying of liver disease, but don't know it. I'm not talking about Skid-Row Sam. I'm talking about Harriet Housewife and Ferdinand the Financial Wizard.

Sure these people can afford medical care; but by the time the symptoms become obvious, it is too late to do anything about the disease. Many of them are not alcoholics either. Some are just hard drinkers who rarely lose control when they imbibe; their drinking is not progressive in nature, and they function without trouble in their home life, social life, and work life. They *die* of liver pathology nonetheless.

Generally speaking, palpation of the liver by a physician is almost worthless. Half the time it's 95 percent guesswork. Body build, the percentage of fat on the person, the stage of cirrhosis — all of these factors can cause errors in judgment. Placing somone on the table and feeling the liver usually leaves the average physician with next to nothing to go on.

Many heavy drinkers play a little game like this: They see a physician about a "cold" or some other physical malady and in the process ask him to feel their liver. The physician has 10 people waiting to see him; and besides, as we said, it is almost impossible to diagnose a cirrhotic liver by palpation. But he thumps him a few times and says, "I don't feel anything too bad there, Jim!" So, Jim leaves, thinking that he has a clean bill of health; and he returns to actively killing off what is left of his liver.

Recently I reviewed a study of 100 patients who had liver biopsies during the treatment phase for their alcholism. These were people who had entered alcoholism treatment centers for their problem. Only six percent had normal livers. The pathology ranged from fatty infiltration of the liver to inactive cirrhosis.

The direct relationship between the amount of alcohol consumed and the amount of cirrhosis sustained has long been known. But it must be understood that just because people consume large amounts of alcohol they do not automatically develop cirrhosis of the liver. I've known men and women who never experienced hangovers — because they are never sober that long — but they have normal livers.

This is the age of chemistry. Take a blood sample and feed it into a machine, and there appears a list of 30 chemical tests that evaluate organ function. They are helpful guides, but for the drinker with liver pathology, they can be very misleading. Fifty percent of the liver can be horribly damaged, and the tests will still show good liver function.

This happens quite often. Jim goes to his physician: "Say, Doc, I'd like to see how my liver is doing." He may have gone through a treatment program and have been told he has extensive damage. That may be the only thing that is keeping him sober. Liver screening tests are performed. Often the physician doesn't know his patient's drinking history. And without benefit of this vital information he says, "Jim, your liver is fine!" Jim celebrates by drinking a double, and ends up seeing the same way.

People are usually astounded to learn that only about 15 percent of alcoholics develop cirrhosis of the liver. They are also surprised to learn that cirrhosis can develop without benefit of a drink. Babies have died of cirrhosis. They do know, however, that the more they drink, the more likely they are to develop cirrhosis. And they should know that switching from spirits to beer is a worthless effort.

Anyone who is doing, or has done, any serious drinking should be aware of the major liver pathologies that elbow flexers usually develop. The three problems are: (1) fatty liver, (2) alcoholic hepatitis, and (3) cirrhosis.

It seems that most drinkers develop fatty livers. Drinking causes the liver to become enlarged and may interfere with function. The liver carries on many functions, and interference with these functions can lead to physical illness. Hepatologists do not agree as to the seriousness of the fatty liver. Many believe that fatty livers progress to subclinical (mild form) alcoholic hepatitis, and then progress to cirrhosis. Some hepatologists have stated that the fatty liver is not all that bad. The definite link between the fatty liver and the progression to alcoholic hepatitis has not been established. My opinion is that a fatty liver is detrimental to one's health.

One of the many functions of the liver is the metabolism of fat. When the liver is preoccupied with detoxification of ethanol, the fat takes up residence in the liver *cell*. It becomes swollen. As the cell swells, so does the liver. It takes on a rounded contour. That's precisely why an enlarged liver does not necessarily spell doom for the alcoholic. It may be relatively innocuous. What happens when drinking stops? With luck, if fat is the only problem, the swollen liver reduces to normal size, and it's business as usual. It takes about six to eight weeks.

As to alcoholic hepatitis, it's easier to talk about it than have it. Up to 30 percent of people with alcoholic hepatitis die with it. These patients are real sick. They have fever, pain, jaundice, edema, vomiting — usually after a fairly prolonged bout with the evil spirits. They do not readily respond to medication. They simply have markedly inflamed livers from the direct toxic effect of alcohol. There are much more pleasant ways to die.

Cirrhosis is a horrible way to go. In its terminal stage, it causes men and women to develop abdomens that resemble eight to nine-month pregnancies, badly swollen legs, yellow skin, yellow eyes, nausea and vomiting, diarrhea, loss of body hair, broken skin vessels, intestinal bleeding. Since the liver can no longer handle protein, ammonia builds up in the blood, and soon the patient doesn't know what hour, day, month, year, century it is. I've seen many patients linger this way for months before they die.

I've also seen patients spend weeks in the hospital, get rid of jaundice and swelling of their gut and legs, leave the hospital, and then drink on the way home. When I make this statement, people seem to think I'm crazy; but it is very true. *People do not understand addiction.* They shake their heads in disbelief. How can people who are literally snatched from the jaws of death by the medical wizardry of a half dozen physicians and dedicated medical personnel go right out and drink? Quite a few never make it past the first bar.

Others are shaken up for a few months. The physician tells patients that they can never drink again or they will surely die. It seldom works. With *treatment* for alcoholism, the patient has a fighting chance for survival. But most of the time, treatment for the real problem is never mentioned.

Scare tactics are essentially worthless when working with addicts. And alcoholics are drug addicts. Oh, patients who survive cirrhotic attacks which send them to the hospital may abstain for a while, but just until their health returns. One of their favorite lines is: "There are more old drunks than there are old doctors!" And down to the bar they go for an hour and a quart. This may sound dismal, but that's the way it is.

I sent a man to a nursing home three months ago. He arrived in the hospital just about as ill as one can be. He was 72 years of age, and apparently he lived by himself in a trailer outside the city for many years. He came by ambulance to the emergency room. His first name was Carl.

Carl had quite a distinguished career. He made a pile of money in his day. He was in "sales" and he must have been topflight. According to his son, Carl had turned down fabulous offers in "management" simply because he loved his "sales" work. A real pro, he knew he could make more money as a sales representative.

Carl's wife was an alcoholic. She died of alcoholism about 15 years ago. Carl was a heavy drinker too, but when his wife was alive, he controlled his drinking because he had to take care of her. When Carl's wife died, he retired. He spent the last 15 years drinking about a quart a day. He took care of his business affairs, making periodic trips. His drinking was not progressive. He *always* drank heavily; he just liked his whiskey. His many friends enjoyed his unusual sense of humor, wit, and they profited from his intellectual stimulation. He never really got into trouble. Carl would probably not be called an alcoholic, but he could certainly qualify as a "hard drinker."

I first saw Carl after he had been in the hospital about a week. Fortunately, he was under the care of a very competent gastroenterologist, who asked that I see him. Carl's abdomen was distended to the point that it resembled a terminal pregnancy. He looked like he wasn't long for this world. He was disoriented, so I couldn't interview him.

I stopped by to see Carl several times over the next several weeks. His cerebration improved. His fluid gradually left. He lost between 20 to 25 pounds. His head cleared up so that he could converse. When I started on the subject of alcohol, he was thoroughly surprised. He genuinely hadn't the slightest notion that his pathology was related to his drinking.

The medical work-up of course pointed to the liver. His serum ammonia was way up, the liver enzymes were elevated, the liver scan was positive, the liver biopsy was positive. For an entire month, he couldn't stand without assistance. He couldn't eat, and he was incontinent of urine and stool. Other than this he was in good shape.

When Carl's head cleared somewhat, all he wanted to do was to get out of the hospital. The gastroenterologist refused permission and insisted on getting him into treatment. Much against his will, he finally agreed; but it was near-gunpoint pressure that convinced him.

Carl's liver was gone. The few viable cells he had left were working overtime. We restricted his protein intake. He received all the medical support possible to bring his liver back. Too much was destroyed. His friends came to see him frequently. Twice, his son flew in from the East Coast to visit him. Alcohol had all but killed Carl, yet I doubt if he ever was an alcoholic. God knows he had been a heavy drinker. To get cirrhosis *all* you need is exposure. Carl definitely got exposed. Three months ago he was transferred to the best nursing home in town. Since money was no problem, he could afford the best. I received word today that Carl was dead.

Of course, not *all* cirrhotic patients develop *enlarged* livers. Through the years, the deposition of collagen (fibrous) tissue in the liver interferes with the blood supply. The liver tends to shrink. Heavy drinkers may be relieved to hear that their livers are not enlarged, but they themselves may be in deep trouble. Many cirrhotic patients bleed to death. They do so because the blood vessels that feed and drain the liver become extremely enlarged as a result of back pressure. If those blood vessels happen to be located in the esophagus or stomach and they break, it's usually a life-or-death situation.

We had a 40-year-old school teacher in our facility a few years ago who was in bad shape, physically and mentally, from alcohol abuse. He had cirrhosis of the liver and what is called "esophageal varicies," which are secondary to the cirrhosis problem. (The esophageal varicies are enlarged veins that show up in the lower third of the tube that runs from the back of the mouth to the stomach.) After a good medical work-up, he was informed of his extensive pathology, which he accepted with the usual horror. Ten days later he said that with the knowledge of the gravity of his illness, he would never drink again. He did not need our help any more. Armed with his self-acclaimed intellectual superiority, and his thorough grasp of his illness, he walked out.

About two weeks later, I received a phone call from the highway patrol. An inquisitive neighbor called them because he hadn't seen our friend for several days. The highway patrolman found him all right. He had been dead for about a week. He had bled to death. There was blood from one end of his trailer-home to the other. Bottles were everywhere. The esophageal veins had ruptured. Many alcoholics die in this manner. It is hardly going out in style.

"Good food protects one from the ravages of alcohol." "I'm not an alcoholic because I eat when I drink." Don't bet your life on those statements! Nutrition *is* immensely important, of course. At one time most of the damage attributed to alcoholism was thought to be due strictly to the lack of nutrition. That "truism" is being exploded. More and more evidence leads back to the direct toxic effect of the substance alcohol.

18

"I'm always able to do my job."

Frank was what is known as a fighter pilot's fighter pilot. Judging him in terms of good, better, or best, he would have to be the best. His story is interesting.

When Frank talked to me, he wanted to make it clear that he didn't blame his problem drinking on the military. He's a very honest, straightforward type of man. I suppose he is one of those rare people who would excel in just about anything he tried. He never went beyond himself, however, looking for an excuse as to why he drank.

Frank readily admits that in his day fighter pilots faced a special challenge. A successful pilot — in the estimation of his peers and superiors — was one who could out-fly, out-fight, and out-drink anyone else in the organization. Most of his contemporaries were able to keep the hard-drinking bouts under some degree of control; but in some the seeds for serious drinking were planted.

Frank spent 25 years in the Air Force. It was official policy that fighter pilots be temperate in their drinking. Through the years, varied regulations were introduced in an attempt to curb or eliminate alcohol consumption. Nonetheless, in the world of fighter pilots, peer pressure encouraged, almost demanded, attendance at "beer calls." There was at least an *informal* policy of boozing. Frank takes pride in comparing himself with the typical fighter pilot of today. When he was a young pilot, he and all the others drank at varying levels and degrees. Now, the great majority do not drink, and the ones who do drink are much more cautious. Frank feels that the competition among young pilots is so great that a drinker would have a difficult time keeping pace. True or not, that is his opinion.

For 25 years, Frank flew hard, fought hard, and drank hard. He was consistently promoted in advance of his fellow officers. He went from Captain, Major, Lieutenant Colonel, and Colonel from below the zone, which is reserved for the top two or three percent in each grade level.

In earlier days, he was quite temperate. He occasionally drank a beer at a party. He progressed through the years to what he considers now as a "light social drinker" — he never became drunk or had hangovers. He seldom exceeded two drinks at a party. With increased rank came increased drinking. As a Lieutenant Colonel, he flew missions in Vietnam. It was during that time that drinking became a daily part of his life. He still never became drunk. He fell into the trap of taking several drinks at bedtime in order to "rest." It was his way of being ready for tomorrow's *big one*. He built up quite a tolerance, while developing a love for both the taste and effects of alcohol.

After Vietnam, he was assigned to the Pentagon. At that time he was a full Colonel. His working hours were from six a.m. to eight p.m. One hour and a half of his day was spent in driving to and from work. With those hours, it would seem difficult to squeeze in drinking time; but when there's a will, there's a way. There was sufficient time for a few drinks before bed; and, of course, Friday and Saturday nights were always available. On those days he got loaded. He felt that with the pressures, he deserved not only a few drinks but a good drunk, if time permitted. In terms of priorities, however, the job was always first.

Frank was assigned to teach air tactics after his stint at the Pentagon. It was quite a switch. His work hours were from eight a.m. to two p.m. All of a sudden there was time for golf and serious boozing. He managed both admirably. Alcoholism was beginning to stir.

Later, he was assigned as Deputy Commander for Operations in a Tactical Fighter Wing. The hours were long, the job demanding. Because he was flying, Frank curtailed his drinking. Flying was always first and foremost. The desire to drink was there, but the job held top priority.

Frank became Vice Wing Commander. He drank moderately at parties, and usually had several drinks at home, from time to time; but his job was not adversely affected. As Vice Wing Commander he received an assignment to an overseas base. This meant splitting up his family, so he chose retirement instead.

Retirement was disastrous. Drinking became daily. He drank to the point of oblivion. The days were filled with much idle time and boredom. He enrolled in graduate school at a university. He completed 24 semester hours with a 3.75 grade point average. He was drunk every day.

In fact, while attending graduate school and compiling excellent grades, Frank managed to get smashed twice a day! He scheduled all his classes in the morning. He was home by eleven a.m. and was drunk by two p.m. He would then take a nap. On rising, he would have a few drinks before dinner. After dinner he drank until he almost passed out; then he would go to bed. He arose at two a.m. and studied until seven a.m. He got drunk twice a day and managed to be a top student. He also developed high blood pressure. Because of the high blood pressure, he was placed on pills. As a matter of fact, he was on five pills a day — two different types of medication.

One fine day, after two years of this glorious retirement, Frank needed more medication. He figured he could see the Flight Surgeon, try to disguise how shaky he was, obtain a refill on the blood pressure medication, get a potassium check, and be back home by twelve-thirty p.m. and be drunk by two-thirty p.m. What he didn't know was that his wife had been to see the Flight Surgeon beforehand. Fortunately for Frank, the Flight Surgeon had attended a medical school where students were instructed in the diagnosis and treatment of alcoholism. Coincidentally, the Flight Surgeon, in addition to being an excellent physician, happened to be a friend of mine and had referred other alcoholics to our facility for treatment. Frank gives that man credit for saving his life.

When Frank saw the Flight Surgeon, he had his blood pressure checked. His heart rate was 160. The physician commented on his excellent record as a Commander. He noted that his reputation in the community was excellent. He also stated that Frank was an alcoholic, and that he had two choices. He could go immediately for treatment or he could die. Outside the door, an officer friend of Frank's was waiting patiently for the verdict. Frank had been set up. He considered his choices and said, "O.K., let's go."

He was admitted at noon. At ten p.m. he had his first convulsion. Convulsions are rare at our facility. Frank realized then that he could have died at home, and he may have. He did manage to bite his tongue badly during the convulsion, but it healed rapidly. He was lucky. Still, it was a nightmare for him.

There's much to learn from Frank's story. One thing to note is that his alcoholism developed in the military. I suppose many alcoholism facilities are similar to ours in that a good percent of our patients are retired military. I know for a fact that the Air Force now has nine main alcoholism treatment and rehabilitation programs in the United States and overseas installations. The Army and Navy have very active treatment centers. The Navy in particular has some outstanding programs.

Retirement is a major problem faced by the military community. It is reasonable to expect trouble when men and women are forced to retire in the early 40s. Many people are not ready to retire at 65, much less 40. Retirement usually calls for an entirely new occupation. People at the top of their profession have to start all over again in another profession! The average man on the street couldn't care less whether ex-military people were colonels or sergeants. It is Mr. or Mrs., or Miss or Ms., Smith now. The job market is not exactly screaming for specialists in hand-grenade throwing or, for that matter, fighter pilots.

The service knows this, and it has initiated programs to alleviate transition; but retirement remains one very large problem. Frank functioned well at his job in the service. His alcoholism was well established however. When he retired, he found himself back in school at 46. No longer did he wear a uniform and bear a title that imposed respect — a blow to his pride. On the other hand, he did have a good military pension, and with no more deadlines, no more pressures, he had all the time in the world to drink. The chemistry is beautiful!

Ask anyone who has ever had anything to do with Veterans Hospitals about alcoholism in the post-military personnel. If the Vets Hospitals refused to treat alcohol-related problems, they would have little to do. Inquire. Many a fine person has nurtured his addiction in the service and had it blossom in retirement.

"If I were an alcoholic, I couldn't do my job!" There is no way that can be true. The average alcoholic has been milking his company for five years before he is forced to do anything about his drinking problem. He just *thinks* he is doing a good job. Some may do a reasonable job, but most just get by. Frank may have functioned at 100 percent toward the end, but I doubt it. Who knows? The facts are that very few alcoholics function well when they are drinking.

Alcohol is metabolized during the night. The price exacted during working hours is profound. The nervous system becomes ragged. Anxiety and depression are common. People who miss a few nights sleep are problems. Alcoholics never sleep well. Hard to live with, they are almost impossible to work with. They inadvertently hurt others. They injure the people they work with, they annihilate their families, they alienate their friends. Oh, they do their jobs, but they are not operating at 100 percent.

Frank told me an interesting incident that happened just after he retired. His wife is a great cook, and they have four growing boys who are very proficient in the knife and fork department. About six months after he retired, the stove malfunctioned. His wife figured it was the thermostat. Frank agreed, and since he was genius caliber, he went down to an appliance store and bought a new one for $45.00. With a drink in one hand and a screwdriver in the other, he went to work. A drunk can do anything, and, of course, Frank was no exception. But alcohol doesn't do much for motor skills. He managed to burn a hole in the frame because he forgot to turn off the master switch.

His boys came home from school and had to finish the job, because several hours had elapsed and many drinks had been consumed. The boys read the instructions and completed the job with the exception of one wire. They asked Frank, and with a thick tongue, he instructed them exactly what to do. The job finished, they threw the master switch, and all the fuses blew. Frank ranted and raved. He tried to take the new, ruined thermostat off, but he was so drunk, he couldn't find the screw slots with his screwdriver. The harder he tried, the worse things got. Totally angry, he said, "The hell with it," and went to bed. The boys told him later it was like a "Laurel and Hardy" movie. He swears his boys will never see him drink again.

People like Frank are usually taking tranquilizers, anti-gout pills, sleeping pills, etc., when they enter treatment. When they leave, they are taking a vitamin and Antabuse, if they choose to take the latter. Much of the medication is useless because the symptoms have developed due to the abuse of alcohol. For instance, Frank was taking five pills for high blood pressure. What obviously was happening was that his nervous system was high as a kite when the blood pressure was taken. There was no booze in the system and, of course, that kicked his blood pressure up. When the blood pressure is up, pills are prescribed. Frank got pills. Of course his physician did not know how much he was drinking; this isn't the type of information most people care to publish.

It is amazing how many alcoholics have on hand pills they don't need. Millions of dollars are spent yearly on superfluous medications to remedy ills caused by alcohol consumption. Medication costs money. It costs money to buy booze. The booze in turn makes the drinker spend more money to control harmful symptoms caused by the alcohol. The physical symptoms caused by alcohol abuse are legion.

Do you know how much money is spent to keep the lid on cerebral damage from alcohol? The amount expended on tranquilizers and sleeping pills alone must be enormous. Anyone who has ever had a hangover knows the consequence of alcohol on the nervous system alone. The head feels like a group of healthy young males had been using it for a game of soccer. The tremor gets harder to disguise. The agitation is a contest all by itself.

Sleeping becomes a joke. What sleep is gotten is almost useless.

Brain damage is probably the common physical problem of alcoholics. Memory loss is almost routine. Coordination problems are routine. A patient walks into a physician's office and says he is nervous and depressed. Agitated all the time, he is unable to sleep. He says he is losing his memory and his coordination isn't good. He may have lost some feeling in his hands and feet.

Do you know what will happen to that patient? If he has hospital insurance, he will be placed in the hospital. Two or three thousand dollars later he'll be told that he has a bad case of humpus-bumpus, and he'll leave with pills for high blood pressure, tranquilizers, and sleeping pills. But nothing will have been prescribed for the fifth he drinks every day. That scene will be repeated many times before the pieces start falling together.

Brain damage can be readily demonstrated by sophisticated tests, which, by the way, are very expensive. But most of the time, alcoholics are far advanced in their disease before indications warrant running the test. Suspicion of brain atrophy from booze can be verified by costly lab work. And tests usually confirm the suspicion.

What worries me are the thousands of men and women who will develop brain damage and die like idiots! Some — on the way back from the bar — simply walk in front of a Mack truck. What distresses me are the million men and women who are mentally slipping — and have been slipping for years — and then they *start* to drink! Their mental deterioration shifts from a jog to a sprint. What bothers me are the nice old ladies and distinguished men who do back flips on their steps because of one drink too many. It is sad to see brothers and sisters — with large families themselves — denying themselves in order to come up with enough monthly cash to keep mother in a nursing home. Mother has been an alcoholic for years and now she's a vegetable — a direct result of her drinking.

It has been hypothesized that 10 to 15 thousand brain cells are lost to the individual every time there is any serious drinking done. It adds up. I've seen hundreds of men and women go through treatment — and not make it. A year later they are back for treatment, and the change is astounding. Physically, they have aged five years, and mentally ten years.

Certainly one of the most common pathologies encountered in medical practice is gastric damage from alcohol. As we have already mentioned, alcohol breaks down a natural protective barrier, so that the stomach lining itself is traumatized. The result is "heartburn," from overproducing acid, which leads to ulcers, which, in turn, leads to bleeding. This eventually leads to surgery, which restores a reasonably good stomach that the alcoholic can ruin again with booze.

Millions of dollars are spent on "putting the fire out" with antacids. "Oh, what a relief it is!"

Not all gastric acidity is caused by booze, but a good percentage of it is. How would you like to pick up the tab for all the gastric surgery being performed this very day on alcoholics who have ruined their guts from overindulgence? And every one of them will be back. Alcoholism which caused the bleeding is seldom treated. Repairing the ulcer is merely fighting a delaying action.

Gut damage, pancreatic damage, large intestine damage, liver damage, esophageal varicies, heart damage, muscle damage — all of these pathologies send patients to the hospital. Hypertension, diabetes, arthritis — any chronic condition is exacerbated by the abuse of ethanol. Recently I heard someone quote a study stating that one of every four beds in metropolitan hospitals is taken up by someone abusing alcohol. I'm not too sure any more that the information is all that "far out."

Yes, alcoholics are able to do their jobs — up to a point. There are millions of "Franks" doing their jobs. Most of them are *not* doing them well. Most are costing their companies a minimum of 25 percent of their salaries yearly. That's a minimum. All those people think they have the rest "fooled."

19

"I drink only to ease my pain."

Alcohol does nothing for pain. As a general statement, this couldn't be more true. I've had hundreds of alcoholics give me the song and dance about how booze kills their pain. "I drink because my back hurts, my head aches, my knee is killing me, my arthritis is acting up, etc." Most of the time, all this represents is an excuse to get crocked.

At one time, alcohol was used as an anesthetic. Before chloroform came into prominence around 1840, it was about the only one around. Technically, of course, *alcohol is an anesthetic.* Pharmacology textbooks list it that way. The problem is that to get a blood alcohol up to the point where it has anesthetic value means flirting with the services of an undertaker, not a physician. Ordinarily, people "pass out" when the blood alcohol goes over 0.3 percent. The old saying that "they were so drunk, they felt no pain" is a myth.

Alcohol is a central nervous system *depressant* drug. Most of the painkilling agents — Demerol, codeine, Darvon, talwin, Percodan, etc. — are also *depressant* drugs. To combine one depressant drug with another depressant drug may spell death. It often does. Booze is a natural for those in chronic pain. They are looking for sedation. Pain causes anxiety and nervousness. Drink enough booze and it will alleviate some of the anxiety. (Give the devil his due.) Alcohol produces sedation. (It sedates some people right out of business for good, at one sitting!)

But alcohol is not an analgesic; it does not provide pain relief. Because it is a central nervous system depressant, it can and does provide sedation much like Phenobarbital and the tranquilizers. That is precisely why it is so dangerous for a physician to prescribe depressant drugs for alcoholics. Patients can get almost the same effect from them as they can from booze. And besides, they feel it's perfectly all right to take pills because their physician wrote the prescription for them. Why spend $6.00 for a fifth when almost the same bang can be gotten out of a bottle of pills? . . . And it's so much more respectable!

Alcohol is classified as an anesthetic because it acts like an anesthetic. That makes sense. Remember when you had that last operation? The anesthetist stands at the head of the table and is the one who puts you to sleep. He/she makes sure you don't get too much or too little of the anesthetic. Without him or her, there would be very little surgery performed. As with all general anesthetics, you go through various stages. The first is euphoria — suddenly you feel like you're on Cloud Nine. Soon you slip into a second stage of hypnosis — not quite asleep, but not conscious either. Then it's off to sleepland. Booze works the same way, and people get to learn to love that effect.

Pain is an extremely subjective matter. People have different thresholds. Two people can receive the same amount of stimulus: one complains of violent pain, the other feels hardly anything.

Probably the best friend alcoholics have is *pain*. That's a strange statement, but think about it. If alcoholics are never allowed to feel the pain resulting from their alcohol consumption, the chances are that they will never quit drinking. Their pain is both physical and mental. Families, employers, friends — these people spend a lifetime not allowing alcoholics to experience the ordinary pain resulting from their drinking. As long as that protective shield is there, why stop? Physicians shield them from physical pain. Wives, husbands, mothers, fathers, uncles, aunts, brothers, sisters, sons, daughters shield them from mental pain — pain they should be allowed to suffer. Pain is the alcoholic's best friend. Without it, he or she is a sad case of walking death. I'm sure few people try to *kill* the alcoholic on purpose, but many do just that under the guise of kindness and charity.

Let me tell you a story about my friend Bill. The first words that he spoke to me after admission were, "I don't belong here. I don't have a drinking problem! I only drink because of my pain." We were off to a good start, Bill and I.

Bill started to drink when he enlisted in the Army. He was 17. He had a few beers now and then, but no problems to write home about. However by age 19, Bill was in trouble. He spent 20 days in jail and had his driver's license yanked for 3 years — this for drunk driving. Needless to say, his Army career was brief.

Bill got married at age 21. He claimed that drinking was not a big problem, but the marriage ended seven years later. Let's accept that. During the two years following his divorce, Bill fell in love with "boilermakers." He talks about his love encounter with "boilermakers" as something comparable to the discovery of the atom bomb. (To those less knowledgeable in the finer arts, a boilermaker is a shot followed by a beer.)

In 1962, Bill remarried. He inherited three children, ages three, four, and six. He also kept the boilermaker habit.

In 1964, Bill came down with a bad case of psoriasis. He was hospitalized six different times over the next three years. The condition became progressively worse. Among other things, his toenails and fingernails fell out. In 1967, he developed rheumatoid arthritis. He spent five months in the hospital for treatment of the psoriasis and arthritis. During those five months, Bill says he was completely immobile. Over the following three years, he was hospitalized nine different times. The drinking also progressed.

In 1970, Bill moved to the desert country. He figured that the weather would help the skin and the arthritis, and his physicians encouraged the move. Besides all that, the drinking problem was getting out of hand, and, as everyone knows, a geographic change heals all. He was heavily into both whiskey and beer at the time. Of course the move did nothing but make the drinking problem worse.

In November of 1972, Bill was hauled off one night to the county hospital in delirium tremens. It was not a pleasant experience. As a matter of fact, it was so horrible that he decided to give up whiskey and just stick with beer. (Great thinking, Bill!) He did his very best to keep his habit to two six-packs a day.

Over the next several years, Bill was convicted of public intoxication and, on two occasions, of driving while intoxicated. He has paid out $500 in court costs and fines. He has also spent about 65 hours in the city and county jails for the above alcohol-related offenses. When confronted about his alcoholism, Bill thought that the whole thing was a joke.

Bill's wife forced him into treatment. She was fed up. He drank all day long and most of the night. He stuck strictly to beer, which, of course, he drank for medicinal purposes — *strictly* because of the "pain." I informed him about alcohol doing nothing for pain, which shocked him at first; but after the shock wore off, he sort of just tolerated *my* ignorance. "Everybody knows booze is good for pain." Obviously, I had been reading the wrong books.

Bill spent about six days denying the fact that he had a problem with alcohol. His wife had problems (not with alcohol), the children had troubles, his arthritis and psoriasis were something to worry about; but, as far as he was concerned, booze was insignificant in his life. He could take it or leave it. After the sixth day, he disappeared from the premises. We called his family and the police. He apparently made a snap decision that he'd rather take it than leave it.

About four days later, Bill showed up again. He staggered when he walked, talked with a thick tongue, and had a glassy look about him; and, of course, he "had not taken a drink since he left the Center!" His wife brought him in. He announced that he was here "just to please her." He'd be willing to take a look at his drinking, and go through the entire three-week program.

It took about one week to get Bill off the "alcohol and pain" kick. After another week of group therapy, a different character emerged. He went to AA meetings every night and even got to like AA. He and his wife had several marriage counseling sessions; and, adding it all up, things looked fairly good. Unfortunately, the three weeks were all too short, and we were all wishing we had another three weeks to work with him. But a different man did leave our Center.

I know for sure that Bill is sober today, and he is an active AA member. It has been only six months, but it's a good start. The home life is 90 percent improved, money is in the bank, and the marriage is solid. Bill not only admits he is an alcoholic, he *knows* it and works at sobriety. He takes Antabuse as added insurance. Only time will tell, but the future is favorable. One thing is certain — there's no more talk about using alcohol for pain.

There are thousands of people who have become addicted to alcohol, using pain as an excuse to drink. For instance, I've known many men and women who become alcoholics because of back surgery. Typically, they have multiple surgeries to alleviate the pain and are given narcotics for long periods of time. They become members of the system — Veterans hospitals, county hospitals, the Industrial Commission, and the Social Security brotherhood. Many never work again. When things get slow, they go in for more surgery. Then, it's back to the pain medication after the surgery; and when the pain pills are cut off, it's into the booze.

No one takes the time to explain that alcohol does nothing for pain; but even if this were done, many wouldn't listen anyway. They get wiped out with pills or booze, or a combination of the two. It's a great excuse to pack it all in and stay drunk. The truly sad thing about many people who become addicted to alcohol through the "alcohol-pain" syndrome is that most of them sort of "back into it." No longer able to work, they have much time on their hands. Money is not abundant but there is a *steady* supply. The switch from pills to booze is subtle. When completed, it sometimes becomes lethal.

Headaches are a real boon to anyone who is looking for an excuse to stay half in the bag. They are a magnificent excuse to jump from Demerol to codeine, to Valium, to Librium, to booze, etc. Some people learn to draw headaches like they draw a gun. "Keep in line or I'll have a headache." The only thing that helps is a drink. (Sure it is!)

There is hardly anything worse for headaches than alcohol. Infrequently, a neurologist will use it for injection near a nerve for the purpose of destroying that specific nerve. Other than that, alcohol only aggravates headaches.

Alcoholics set themselves up for a lifetime of headaches *because of* their drinking. Alcohol sedates, but when it wears off psychomotor agitation takes over, and its price is high. Alcoholics take tons of aspirin, and many contribute two thirds of their stomachs to the pathology lab because of bleeding. That doesn't make much sense, does it? Yet, many people get hooked on ethanol because they think it will help their headaches.

Cross-addiction of alcohol with pain pills, tranquilizers, sleeping pills, etc. is an alcoholic's nightmare. One addiction is bad enough. Alcohol does nothing by itself to relieve pain, but it can cause unbelievable complications.

20

"I don't hide bottles."

The first time I saw Paul, he was sunning himself in a lawn chair and shaking like a leaf. He tried to drink a glass of water and spilled it down the front of his shirt. The tremors were bad. He couldn't even find his mouth with a fork. When I asked him how he felt, he told me he was "fine," and he wanted to know how the hell he could get out of our facility. He said he did not have a drinking problem. Our place was nice, but it obviously wasn't for him.

Paul couldn't walk for about three days. He was in his late forties and looked twenty years older. His face was bloated, the complexion mottled, legs swollen, blood pressure elevated, heart rate about 140. When I informed him that in my opinion he was dying of alcoholism, he repeated what I hear so often: "There are more old drunks around than old doctors!" Even in the alcoholic fog, he had a sense of humor.

Paul didn't convulse but he came close to it. He spent 21 days trying to get out of our facility. He called every friend he knew. Twice each day, he begged his wife to come and get him. He steadfastly denied ever having had a drinking problem. At least 20 times he told me that alcoholics *hide bottles.* He never hid bottles, therefore he was not an alcoholic. It must have been a week before he could light his own cigarettes. He couldn't eat; he couldn't sleep. He needed a drink badly.

In the course of the medical work-up, we discovered advanced liver pathology. His liver-function tests were horrible. His liver scan exhibited an enlargement of the liver. A liver biopsy came back showing alcohol hepatitis and advanced cirrhosis. When Paul was informed of these facts, he thought we must have gotten his biopsy mixed up with one of the *alcoholics. His* liver was fine. "There must be some mistake, you see; only alcoholics have bad livers!" Alcohol was no problem with his home life, his work life, or his social life. His wife might have a drinking problem, but not he . . . so says Paul.

The family came to see him. His teen-age kids avoided him like he had a social disease. In spite of vigorous confrontation, he denied everything. He would listen to no one. He only wanted out; nothing else made the slightest bit of sense to him. AA was being shoved down his throat! It might be O.K. for the drunks, but he could handle what little drinking he did. AA was "for the birds." He refused to take Antabuse, but he did agree that anyone who had a problem should take it for a while. He genuinely felt sorry for the "drunks" in our facility.

Paul had a good job in a small city as an executive in the city manager's office. He was literally fired because of his drinking problem. His family knew it. Everyone knew it but Paul. It wasn't his fault, according to him. It was all some sort of ghastly nightmare! "The whole thing was a horrible mistake." His family was almost destitute. His drinking became so bad prior to admission that he was placed in a local hospital. His physician recognized Paul's condition, and referred him for treatment. He was dying of alcoholism at 46 years of age.

Paul as a teen-ager was an all-around athlete, excelling at football and baseball. He had his first drink *after* the final football game when he was 18. It was wine. An Italian buddy of his had ripped off his father. Apparently the friend's father made his own wine and kept it in his cellar. When Paul's buddy stole the wine, he neglected to turn off the spigot all the way. Ten gallons of wine had leaked out on the cellar floor before the father discovered the disaster. Both boys were punished. Not an auspicious start for Paul.

One thing was apparent with Paul's early drinking. He could hold his drinks. He always seemed to be able to drink more than the others, yet still drive everyone else home. He joined the Air Force after high school and married while in the service. His drinking was relatively "social." There was the occasional "drunk," but nothing of any consequence.

Out of the service, Paul got a job with an engineering firm. He went to night school and started moving up in the firm. Along with the promotions, he developed an ulcer. His physician told him the ulcer was due to nerves, coffee, and beer — in that order. He suggested switching to bourbon and water. Scotch was all right too. His two worst enemies soon became "two Scotchmen, *Haig and Haig.*"

As the years went by, promotions continued, and with them the inevitable business luncheon meetings. Martinis before lunch became a ritual and, of course, before the evening meetings also. Then there was always the "nightcap." There were times Paul was too drunk to walk, so he drove. By some minor miracle, the law didn't catch up with him. He readily admits now that his guardian angel put in a lot of overtime.

The usual geographic move took place in the early 1960s. He landed a good job with a State agency in the Southwest, and, as usual, thought everything would come up roses because of the change of friends and scenery. For a while, it worked. His drinking was restricted to a few before dinner and a couple on weekends.

The State job required traveling. Paul began drinking at meetings and conventions, and blamed it on missing his wife and five children. After ten years of boozing on the State, he figured that the traveling was the real source of his problem, so he accepted another job in a small city.

The drinking problem on the new job became worse instead of better. Not too surprisingly, financial difficulties began to arise. He found himself drinking in the morning just to get started. The drinking became continuous. His health deteriorated steadily. Paul was brought to the hospital. His diagnosis was officially "nervous fatigue." After a week there, he was spirited off to our Center. That's when I first met my friend Paul. He couldn't hold a glass without spilling the contents because of the "shakes."

When he left our facility, he genuinely wished us the best. Sure, he might have had a drinking problem, but he was by no means an alcoholic. Just to keep his family happy, he stated that he would not drink again. The liver problem shook him up a bit, and the threat of dying with cirrhosis of the liver made an impression. He went home saying he was genuinely through with drink. "I don't miss it anyway! I never needed it!" He continued to repeat that he "never hid a bottle." To him, that was the cardinal sign of alcoholism. He was through drinking though, once and for all! He lasted about two weeks.

Previously, Paul never drank on the job. He soon was drinking in the morning again, and on the job too. It became necessary to drink in the morning because of the shakes. A combination of political pressure and his drinking caused him to lose his job. For a month and a half he drifted around the state doing consultant work, and sinking deeper and deeper into the alcoholism quicksand. His wife and 19-year-old son finally got fed up and forced him to come back for treatment.

It took about an hour of arguing to get Paul to the point of admitting himself the second time. He presented quite a case, stating that he'd come in only if he wouldn't have to go to those "loathsome AA meetings, with those disgusting phonies, etc." (Paul has a beautiful disposition when he's drunk.) He got up to leave numerous times, and several other times the exit door was pointed out to him. He finally decided to give us a break and he stayed.

The medical work-up showed *progressive* advancement of the liver pathology. The liver destruction had progressed to the point of no return. After three weeks his ammonia was still elevated in the bloodstream. He also exhibited more coronary pathology than he had previously shown. All this in four and one half months!

The violent tremulousness stopped after about two weeks. No longer playing the role of Scrooge, Paul turned on to the program during the next week. He not only went to AA; he got to like the meetings and started to listen. He came to admit that he was an alcoholic, and he began to castigate some of the phonies who were in treatment with him. On deciding that he needed Antabuse, he felt that anyone who didn't take it as insurance for a few years while learning AA was a "complete fool." If he could carry life insurance, health insurance, a spare tire in his car, then insurance against that first drink at the cost of a mere eight cents a day sounded pretty good!

When Paul left for home he was a different person. The last thing he said was that he would attend an AA meeting that night in his hometown. Unless Paul is the number-one "con" artist of this decade, he'll make it — not only to that meeting but to meetings for the rest of his life. He just might turn into another *St. Paul.*

St. Paul was the number-one persecutor of the Christians before a bolt of lightning knocked him to the ground. The Lord set him straight as he lay there, and St. Paul did a 180-degree turn. He became the number-one promoter of Christianity. Maybe this Paul will do the same for AA. In helping others, he'll help himself. If he promotes AA with one half of the energy he expended in fighting it, he just might rescue half the county.

A few lessons emerge from this story. They are fairly obvious, but let's look at some of them.

1. The fact that he pinned the diagnosis of alcoholism on not hiding bottles is a tragic joke. However it was no joke to him. Paul is intelligent but "thick-headed" — in the sense that waving a magic wand would hardly suffice to dislodge an idea. He succumbed to the "Irish virus" probably 10 years ago, and it has been downhill ever since. The alcoholic frequently is the last to get the message, and Paul was no exception to this rule. I've seen many men and women shake like they are in

an earthquake when withdrawing from alcohol. Yet with the utmost sincerity they'll tell me that alcohol is no problem in their lives. Anyone could see — even from 100 yards — that Paul was a "dyed-in-the-wool" alcoholic. He was hanging on by his fingernails with the bit about hiding bottles.

2. He would not believe he had liver pathology even after blood function tests, liver scan, and liver biopsy showed the seriousness of his condition. He felt I was pulling his leg, just to convince him to stop drinking. By the way, some physicians do try this tactic. The wife calls the doctor and says, "Waldo is killing himself with drinking and it is tearing up the family." The doctor says, "Send Waldo in!" Dr. Smith does some liver work-up, and tells Waldo that his liver is bad and he must stop drinking. Waldo's liver is probably better than the doctor's, but the "scare" tactic is in force. Waldo stays away from the booze for two months. Then he starts in slowly, and within another month he's in worse shape than ever. Scare tactics are practically useless in the case of addiction; at best, they are very short-termed. Addicts don't scare easily. The drug is number one. All else is of secondary importance — job, family, everything and everyone.

3. Paul didn't just dislike AA; he hated it. To him, AA meant admission of alcoholism. Paul had an executive position. He was a professional. To him, alcoholics were skid-row bums. He could not relate to this concept. He

would not relate to it. It was useless to tell him that his concept of alcoholism is false and that the skid-row person represents only two to three percent of all alcoholics.

It is easy to see where he was coming from and why he hated AA. Many people choose to die rather than admit to being alcoholic. Their pride is too great. Pride can work for us or against us. In this instance it becomes deadly. Those who freely choose to die rather than accept the fact that they are alcoholics need to be educated. They need to sit with other men and women of their caliber and status who have gone through the same thing. They need to share their feelings, fears, anxiety, and depression. They need the comfort and help that is available when a crisis strikes after months and years of sobriety. They need a philosophy of life to help them grow. They need AA more than anything else in the world.

4. Paul had the good fortune to consult a physician who knew he was in bad shape. Recognizing this, he referred him to a Center that specializes in the treatment of alcoholism. Many physicians do not do this. For many reasons, they shuffle the alcoholic in and out of hospitals for years and years *before* they refer them for treatment. Hospitals are bulging with alcoholics being treated under the guise of phony diagnoses. Paul got a break. His physician was not only sharp but he was ethical and humane. He was more interested in his patient than his pocketbook. The facts are that even the special treatment center

where Paul was sent, the Center I represent, *failed.* Paul didn't make it; therefore, we failed. We fail quite a bit, and our program is of such quality that people descend on us from all over the country. (On the very day I wrote this story about Paul we received a patient who traveled over 3,000 miles to enter our alcoholism treatment facility.) Still we failed. It keeps us humble. The 21 days were not wasted, however.

5. He lost his job. The primary reason was his drinking. Alcoholics lose jobs with regularity. But sometimes they don't. Much depends on the type of job they have, how many "friends" cover, strength of the union, company alcoholism policy, etc. If Paul hadn't lost his job, he'd probably still be out there trying to prove he can drink socially. He got a break. He got fired. The man who fired him might have saved his life.

6. He was up against it financially. As a matter of fact, he declared bankruptcy. That frequently happens with alcoholics. Financial problems create a crisis that frequently makes alcoholics do something about their alcoholism. If they are rescued by family, friends, others, this only permits them to continue on their merry way of killing themselves with their drug. Through pressure from his wife and son, Paul came back for another try at treatment, but he wasn't exactly *pleased* about coming back.

7. His initial treatment didn't take. No one would have given a nickel for his chances. Only the very strong stay sober. He would have nothing to do with AA, and Antabuse was "simply not needed." He needed no *one* or no *thing.* In his mind, sobriety was simple: Just don't drink any more! In short, Paul was *nowhere.* He was unwilling to change anything. Many people do not make it the first time around. Those of us in this work are not happy about that; but we try to give everyone 100 percent, and hope for the best. We try our best; but, unfortunately, our best is not always enough. The work is not easy but the rewards are great.

8. He stayed away from alcohol only two weeks. That, of course, was no surprise. If he had gone out bursting with zeal for AA and determined to take the Antabuse for two years, his chances would still be limited. Many do all the things they are supposed to . . . for a while. They get lazy in a hurry. By not being active in AA, they get their priorities all mixed up. Their thinking gets scrambled, and people don't stay sober that way. Sobriety is *work.* Paul, of course, didn't even try.

9. Four and a half months later he was in worse shape than ever. That usually happens with most alcoholics. Alcoholism is a progressive disease. The frightening thing about Paul was the swiftness of his deterioration. A repeat liver scan exhibited progression. In my mind, Paul is a dead man if he resumes his

drinking. His nervous system is shot. His digestive system is damaged. Some brain atrophy has to be there. I believe Paul was unusual from this point of view. I'm used to seeing people deteriorate physically from alcoholism. I see people age 10 years in 12 months. Men and women come in for treatment looking like they are 70, but they are actually in their 50s. I was shocked to see the remarkable progression of Paul's disease.

10. He drank heavily for a long time before going over the line. Some go very fast. Most alcoholics do not get that way overnight. Paul again was no exception. He drank heavily in the service. He drank heavily in the business world — at lunches and at cocktail parties. His drinking problem got steadily worse.

11. He took the "geographic change." Alcoholics do this all the time — new school, new job, new home, new friends, new bar, new occupation — always expecting their drinking problem to disappear. It never seems to work out.

12. In early years, he developed an ulcer. His physician suggested a switch from martinis to whiskey and water. That's like telling a barbiturate addict to change from Nembutal to Tuinal.

13. When he was hospitalized, the diagnosis was "nervous fatigue." On the East Coast, someone once did a study on emergency-room patients. (The following facts are not necessarily true everywhere, but they were

well founded in this instance.) He found that when a patient entered being poorly dressed, with no hospitalization insurance, and no family with him, the diagnosis of the emergency room physician was "alcoholism." If the person was fairly well dressed, had hospitalization insurance, and perhaps a family member along, *that* person suffered from "anxiety, gastritis, depression, nervous tension, cephalalgia, etc." Both reeked of booze, but only one was an "alcoholic." Paul was a city executive. He had "nervous fatigue." (Sure he did!)

14. He had to be brought back into treatment, practically in chains. How can this be? How could a proven alcoholic be back four and one half months later, shaking like a leaf, having lost another job, surrounded by a pleading family, and still be in a state of denial? It happens every day. Thank God, Paul's wife and son didn't back down. If they had, the chances are that the only thing left of him would be an insurance policy. With a little luck and a lot of hard work, he may have 10 to 20 good years left in him.

15. After a week or so, Paul changed his tune about AA. Many people do this. They try it their way, get punched around some more, then take a real look at AA. They finally take the sunglasses off and take an honest look at AA. They find many happy fellow alcoholics hanging in there helping each other to make it. After a few years of study, soul-searching,

assisting others, and putting their acts together, they get some real insight into just how beautiful life can be. They join the finest people in the world.

16. Paul became almost evangelical about AA. That's the good news. The bad news is that some people get "burned out" too quickly. They want to save the world. Did you ever notice this about people who just gave up cigarettes? Most are standing around adjusting their halos, and giving everyone else the business about smoking. Some become a pain very quickly. I like to see a little fanaticism about AA at first — but not too much. Alcoholics who burn out quickly do not keep their sobriety. Every alcoholic should have an *AA sponsor,* and every recovering alcoholic should lean on that sponsor with regularity. An AA sponsor helps the alcoholic to keep his/her feet on the ground. A good sponsor can be of immense value.

We can ferret out much information from Paul's life. Good listeners learn a great deal from other people, and they provide a great service in allowing others to ventilate. If we can get people talking, very often they provide solutions for their own unique problems. Many people just need a kind ear. Communication skills do not come easily. Some have them, some don't. Most people need to work at them.

Some alcoholics are very shy and introverted. In AA, they often do not stay that way because they are forced to communicate. A great asset of AA is the fact that there are so many different types of meetings. Often it is just a matter of shopping around to find comfortable groups. It takes effort and it takes time. I love to see our people involved with *several* AA groups. That way they never become bored with the same meeting and the same people. It can happen.

21

"I drink only to gain self-confidence."

Ed is a personable young man in his mid thirties. On seeing him rushing around the hospital, stethoscope protruding from his coat pocket, you would have to say, "Now there's a competent doctor who looks like he knows what he is doing and knows where he is going!" If you sat down and talked with him, you'd probably say to yourself, "Now here's a kind, knowledgeable, intelligent, interested young physician." You'd like him immediately. I know for a fact that all those descriptive adjectives fit him perfectly. He is also a drug addict and an alcoholic.

Alcoholism and poly-drug abuse affects physicians as readily, if not more so, than the rest of the populace. Ed is addicted to alcohol and other mind-altering drugs, including narcotics. He has not had a drink, pill, or injection for over four years, and he radiates an inner peace that few physicians are able to generate. He is obviously a happy man.

Ed came from a loving family. As a youth, his most significant characteristic was shyness and the usual lack of social skills that go along with it. When he began to date in high school, he felt enormously ill-at-ease. In his senior year, he discovered alcohol. A few beers and he suddenly became a *complete* person. He describes the sensation as "finding a part of me that had always been missing." "Booze plus me equaled a complete person!" He was a good student, but nothing came easily. In short, he worked very hard.

In college, alcohol began to interfere with his studies and ambitions. He joined a fraternity, and the more time he devoted to drinking and socializing, the less time he devoted to study. His grades began to show it. It suddenly became necessary to put himself on a rigid schedule of *no* drinking during the week. He confined his boozing to Saturdays and Sundays. He held to this pattern through college and into medical school.

In the second year of medical school, Ed made a second marvelous discovery — amphetamines. At the time, amphetamines were used extensively for weight reduction, and samples of the medication were readily available. He used them to stay awake while studying for exams. He found that even though they are technically *stimulating* drugs, they gave him the same euphoric effect of "completeness" that he got from alcohol. With more partying, he began to be bothered by hangovers and occasional blackouts. By taking "speed" together with alcohol he increased the amount he could drink, and this made his hangovers more bearable the following days.

This too set a pattern: He took amphetamines during the week, and amphetamines plus alcohol on the weekends. He also started to develop headaches from the amphetamines, and had to use Darvon or codeine to stay on top of them. Since amphetamines jangle the nervous system, he began to develop tremors. A shaky hand is hardly what a physician needs, so he started taking Librium, Valium, or barbiturates. Sleep became almost impossible. Barbiturates plus alcohol solved this problem.

Ed's life became a nightmare of fine-tuning with chemicals. Alcohol was just one of many drugs employed in balancing the physical machinery. Mood and energy levels were programed by what was in store the following day.

Medical school, marriage, and internship were all negotiated, and, at last, he found himself in General Practice. For the first time, he had access to injectables — amphetamines, Demerol, morphine, talwin, etc. He figured he would use them only in particular circumstances where he would be subjected to a great deal of pressure. It wasn't very long before he was a heavy user of both injectable amphetamines and narcotics.

Ed had a partner. The partner wasn't dumb, and he wasn't blind. He began to get suspicious and make noises. Ed was no dunce either. He purposely precipitated arguments, caused trying situations, etc. Soon he created enough heat to give him an excuse to terminate the partnership and leave town. True to the nature of the disease, he hung the whole thing on the partner. He even believed it himself. The poor partner was bewildered.

The "geographic cure," of course, was no solution. A new practice in a new state solved nothing. His reduced drug intake caused anxiety and depression. Relief came only with increased use of the alcohol and other drugs. Then the heavy price of withdrawal had to be paid. As usual, matters just got worse. His new medical partners soon began to get nervous. One day he overdosed on Darvon while in the office and went into convulsions. They shipped him off to a psych ward.

There, he was informed that his problem was due to anxiety-depressive neurosis. He couldn't argue because he was truly anxious, and who in his right mind would not be depressed? He was discharged from the unit after four weeks, still viewing the world with hopelessness and fear. He faced two facts at this juncture of his life: 1) As a physician, he could not function properly while using chemicals; 2) he could not function at all without them.

Feeling certain that he could control them, he stopped all drugs except one. He drank a bottle of wine every day. And this worked for a while. Then he decided to take a psychiatric residency — to find out why he drank. He was spending a small fortune on psychiatrists anyway, and getting nowhere. By getting into the field itself, he felt he would solve his problem. Accepted for training as a psychiatrist in one of the most prestigious psychiatric centers on the East Coast, he lasted six months.

Before leaving the residency, the director of training encouraged him to see a psychiatrist friend of his. He went. To Ed's surprise, this psychiatrist sat down and told him about *his* booze problem, and how he beat the rap with Alcoholics Anonymous. He even set up a meeting for him with AA.

The day of the meeting Ed couldn't get out of bed. Afraid to get up, he lay there with the covers over his head. Petrified with fear, he had to take amphetamines to get out of bed.

The meeting was composed entirely of physicians. Each told his story of drugs or alcohol, and usually both. Unfortunately, Ed was out of his skull on "speed," so he got little out of it. He went to two other meetings with the psychiatrist; both times he was stoned. Finally, he decided that he needed inpatient hospital treatment.

Checking into a small hospital in another section of the country, he stayed there for six weeks. AA was pounded into him. When he left, he had a powerful force to help keep him straight. Determined to use it, he attended AA regularly. That was four years ago. At present, he is not just *sober;* he has quality sobriety, and it shows.

Ed says that living without chemicals has become a joy. There are frustrations; he still has his bad days. Following the principles of AA is what makes his life worth living. Accepting the fact that he owes his life to AA, he'll spend the next 30 years helping thousands of others gain sobriety and lead chemical-free lives. He's a much better man than most. He's a much better physician than most. He's a much better father than most. He's a much better husband than most. Why shouldn't he have an inner glow?

Again, we can learn something from Ed's story:

1. Ed was an introvert.
He is still somewhat of an introvert, but AA has done much to change that. He found that booze gave him more confidence, and he was more "whole" when he had a few drinks. That effect as years went by caused him to become addicted to the drug alcohol. Simple, isn't it? It happens to thousands every day.

2. He realized that drinking and studying do not mix.
Without taking definite steps to curtail his drinking he would not have made it through college. If he hadn't had the will power to restrict the drinking to weekends, he would never have graduated. Ambition fired the will power. Many a promising premed student fails because of drinking.

3. He got into amphetamines in medical school.
Pop a pill and most people can study all night.

Some have to pop pills to keep awake for the exams too. After exams, they sleep for 24 hours. The effect of these pills is similar to that of booze. But the two drugs are pharmacological opposites. Alcohol *depresses* the inhibitory centers of the brain, thereby turning the introvert into a semiextrovert. Unfortunately, it made Ed an entirely different person. Amphetamines *stimulate*. Without tolerance, they'll blow your head off. Both provide transient euphoria. Both are attractive drugs. Both are seductive, which is where the danger lies.

4. One drug leads to another.
Alcoholics are in and out of the doctor's office, in and out of hospitals, in and out of innumerable physical troubles. Alcohol abuse leads to other drug abuse. And it is the same with amphetamine abuse. Tranquilizers are needed to stop the shakes, sleeping pills are needed to get some sleep, amphetamines are used to get the motor running after a hangover from booze. Sedatives are used to replace sedatives . . . so the nightmare lingers.

5. How could he study all those years and actually go into medical practice without being recognized as an addict by his fellow physicians?
Answer: Very easily. Physicians, as a rule, know next to nothing about addiction. I can make that statement with some authority, because until the last several years, I knew absolutely nothing. (After ten years, I wonder

how much I really know now.) There is almost no training in medical school about alcoholism or drug addiction; and this in spite of the fact that the average physician sees at least one alcoholic every day. Besides, Ed — smart as he was — played the system like a finely tuned violin.

6. He opted for geographic change.
If there is one consistent finding in alcoholics, it is their resort to the geographic cure. Ed picked fights with his partner in order to precipitate a move. This is a typical gesture of an addict.

7. He was shuffled off to a psych ward after convulsing in his office.
The diagnosis was anxiety-depressive neurosis. But Ed was an obvious alcoholic and a poly-drug abuser. The anxiety-depression was secondary to those conditions.

8. His psychiatric treatment was unsuccessful.
No treatment is 100 percent effective, but psychiatric treatment for an alcoholic is almost useless — that is my opinion. I have seen psychiatrists help alcoholics *after* they have some quality sobriety, but seldom before.

9. He decided he would go into a psychiatric residency.
He wanted to find out why he drank. By getting into the field itself, he felt he could solve his problem. But this didn't work out either.

10. His psychiatric residency ended in six months.

Ed simply could not function. His boss referred him to a psychiatrist who really knew what he was doing. The man tried to get him into AA. It didn't take, but he tried. Ed needed inpatient help.

11. He was sent to an alcoholism facility to get help.

The facility kept him six weeks and impressed on him the importance of AA. They did a good job. And, overcoming his pride, Ed did a good job on himself. So many intellectuals seem to think that AA is for the common herd. But they themselves are the sickest of the sick.

12. He got well.

Sure Ed got well, but he works every day at it. It's been four years, and he still goes to a couple of AA meetings a week. Forty years from now, he'll still be going to them. Forty years from now, he'll probably still be getting a lot from AA, and giving a lot in return.

Staying sober is something like staying in good physical shape. We do not develop our physiques by sitting back on our haunches and watching the world go by. If I asked my average patient to run 10 miles, very few could do it. But if they had been running 10 miles regularly, they could do it with no strain. All alcoholics run into stress periodically. If their guard is up and if they are ready for that stress, they can handle it. AA helps prepare them for that stress. It's cheap, it's effective, and it's everywhere. It's the AA way of staying in shape.

For years, I've been hearing countless reasons why people cannot get involved with AA. Invariably, the ones with the loudest voices and persistent excuses are the ones who cannot stay sober. Ed made it through AA. He is one of millions. "Stick with the winners!" If I sound like I'm on commission with AA, then so be it. As a nonalcoholic, I can afford to be objective. I was impressed when I first became involved in alcoholism treatment. After 10 years I'm more impressed than ever.

**For more information about alcohol
and the disease of alcoholism, read:**

America's Worst Drug Problem: Alcohol
by Richard L. Reilly, D.O.

An interesting examination of the drug alcohol
and the disease alcoholism. Dr. Reilly explains
what alcohol is, how it affects your body and
mind, and what follows the progression from
"social drinker" to alcoholic. Dr. Reilly is the
full-time medical director at West Center, Tucson
General Hospital's rehabilitation facility for alcoholics and drug patients. *128 pages, $1.75.*

Alcohol and the Family:
Three Sure Ways to Solve the Problem
by Father Frank, C.SS.R.

Every year, more and more people fall victim to
the disease of alcoholism. It's a problem that
reaches beyond the individual alcoholic to affect
family, friends, and associates. This book offers
hope and help. It explains why the three
organizations that have helped so many —
Alcoholics Anonymous, Al-Anon, and Alateen —
have been successful. The first organization
confronts the problem of the alcoholic; the
other two, the problems of the family. The
message of this booklet is that "there is someone
who can help." *64 pages, $1.50.*

Order from your local bookstore or write to:
Liguori Publications
Book and Pamphlet Department
One Liguori Drive
Liguori, Missouri 63057

*(Please enclose payment on orders under $10;
add 50¢ for postage and handling.)*